Freedom, My Way

The Journey and Revelations of A Black Man in America

MICHAEL ABDULLAH KHEOP

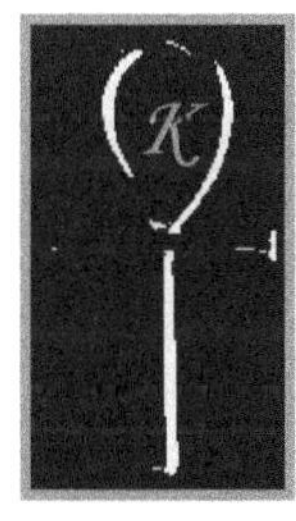

Kheop Publishing

Kheop Publishing
26500 West Agoura Road
Suite 102-435
Calabasas, CA 91302

Copyright © 2001, 2010 by Michael Kheop

www.kheop.com

All rights reserved. No part of this book may be reproduced or transmitted in any form or by any means, graphic, electronic, or mechanical, including photocopying, recording, taping or by any information storage or retrieval system, without the permission in writing from the publisher.

Composed and Edited by Meru Kheop

Cover and Page Layout Design by Meru Kheop

Original Photos by Meru Kheop

Originally published 2001.

PRINTED IN THE U.S.A.
Reprint 2010, 2011

ISBN 13: 978-0-6153-8099-5

ISBN 10: 0615380999

"I've spent much of my life being a revolutionary. At least, that's what I always aspired to be. I read a quote from an ancient outlaw, he said, "All revolutionaries are dead men on furlough." When I read this, I knew I was very close to being what I've aspired to become most of my life. I've felt dead inside for so long that I didn't know if I was even living on the outside.

I was starting to comprehend the opposition law of the universe. If I felt so dead, someone or some people were feeling very much alive. I always felt the life of a revolutionary was a tormented life, but I thought it was as close to happiness that a conscious man could hope for. I was wrong, grossly wrong.

My knowledge of the universe was so limited, my wisdom so shallow. I had only a vague comprehension of the nature of things. My life had been so filled with hate that I couldn't perceive anything of a higher nature."

CONTENTS

Part II

FOREWORD

There are days when the Sun shines on Earth and I feel a burst of energy flow through my entire body. I am lifted higher. My thoughts are positive, and I am inspired to do all the things that I know I am capable of doing. Things that will change life as we know it. My husband, partner and friend – My King - Michael Abdullah Kheop – does for me what the Sun does for the Earth, *raise*. At some point in one's evolution you must make a choice to believe or leave. At that moment when fear attempts to completely overtake the senses, one must release all negative thought patterns and accept eternity. When my moment arrived, I kept envisioning myself standing tall and erect, with dignity and confidence, alongside the Sun. I cried tears of extreme joy for I made it. I made it to the other side. Those who have know what I speak.

On a warm October Sunday evening in 1999, I was invited to attend a gala with friends from the mother continent, Africa. This gala was to mark the closing of a week long conference on Slavery held at New York University and The Schomberg Center for Black Research. On the prior evening, Dr. Leonard Jeffries, one of our most fearless scholar warriors whom my mother traveled with to Ghana some years earlier, invited me to the

John Henrik Clarke House on Convent Avenue. He and other scholars from Africa and the U.S. were forming a community university. When Sunday afternoon rolled around I decided to visit the Clarke House instead of partying at a gala.

It was at the John Henrik Clarke House that I met my King, and I haven't looked back since, only ahead. Michael Abdullah Kheop is a bright light that shines brightly, and his words are in unison with his actions.

I am a woman, a feminine spirit that has traveled many, many places, and my awareness of my own power is high. I created Michael as he created me. I am a wife and a mother. I am proud of my husband for we are representative of each other. Acknowledging his greatness is not ignoring my own. He is great because I am. We need each other. Oftentimes our personal relationships are built on a weak foundation because we are individually weak.

My husband taught me that what we call God is inside us. Religion has us focused outside ourselves, therefore separating ourselves from the Universe - God. We are not separate from the cosmic circle of life. Laws, Justice, and Punishment are impositions to spirit - to nature - to Creation. Humans are the only creation that function this way, and it is destructive all the way around.

The destruction will not cease unless we who were first placed on this planet begin to embrace being what we really are. This is not going to be easy, but I know it will be done. Each of us who was born and raised in the United States has been influenced by factors outside ourselves. As one becomes more aware of how detrimental these influences are on our spirit, it becomes more challenging to evolve past it. Creation continues, and the babies born in recent years, and those that are to be born in the years to come, must be given the Truth.

We are responsible for cultivating our world, peacefully. Let's discover who we really are from our hearts. It may be a little painful, but once past the pain, it is the most ecstatic feeling.

To my Sisters, I would like to say that our men mirror us, yet they are our opposites at the same time. We are the same - in spirit. Those that are truer to their nature are active, commanding, concentrated and fiery. Those of us who are truer to our nature are gentle, tranquil and magnetic. One is not weaker than the other - in spirit, which is our force, our strength. It is a dance we do when we evolve together. Brothers and sisters interfere with "balance" when one decides it doesn't need the other. Our ancient ancestors were closer to it than we are, but it is in us. We can do this.

Listen to my husband's words, and feel his vibe.

Peace, Love & Light,
Meru Nombeko Aisha Kheop

I dedicate this book to all my brothers and sisters around the world who are asking questions about the world we live in. Keep asking and keep trying.
It's our time NOW.

INTRODUCTION

My name is Michael Kheop. I wrote the book you have in your hand. It is not an autobiography, but some thoughts on paper I wrote over the course of 4 years. Part 2 I wrote more recently. My wife, Meru Kheop, encouraged me to write down and publish this book for you the reader. These are stories of my life as an outlaw, for I have been an outlaw in the country of my birth since birth.

So much racism and evil tricks are hurled at we Black children in America. Yet, we grow strong from the trials and tribulations. We fight however we can, but we forever bang for greater freedom and liberty from a nation that views our freedom as the beginning of the destruction of this nation we call home, America.

I am 33 years of age as I write this intro. The book you are holding is not a definition of me, but a part of me. The thoughts and feelings I've written are painful at times, and funny other times. Life hasn't been one long tragedy for me, but a wonderful journey. My anger is real, and my will to move beyond all of the confusion is deeply rooted in me.

My wish for this book is that it will give some light to all those who will come after myself. I wrote this so that others who have lost their way can use my life as a road map to find their way. I haven't lived an American dream, but I have certainly lived my dreams and aspirations to the fullest. I encourage you the reader to follow me in this. Live your life, be yourself, for that is what the world needs. The world is yours and mine. There is room enough in this world for all of us to shine. I know racism is terrible, but the world is big and your soul is infinite. Find a way out. Not out of the black community, but out of the mental prison that evil men and women erected over 500 years ago. It isn't easy, but possible. Because you, me, we are already working ourselves out of this mess. I wrote these words for you, and your reading is proof that we are rising.

This book is about the process of Michael Kheop doing Michael Kheop. By doing, I mean making myself, creating a new man. A man who all the generations of Black folk who come after me will respect and acknowledge as a truthful and soulful man. It has been a struggle to come this far, and by no means is my struggle over. So, please read and enjoy my working me out to help us out.

Life, Health and Strength,
Michael A. Kheop

PART I

THE CREATOR

I believe and have faith in the goodness of creation. I see an order in the universe that overwhelms all my senses. Earth, to me, is one ball of activity, and my life as well as yours is an active part of God's creation.

Now, what confused me for so long was the question of good and evil. I wondered how could something so all good, all-powerful, and all wise as the Creator, create evil?

To answer this question, I studied long and hard. I contemplated every new discovery that my studies uncovered. I asked questions of those I felt could give me an answer. I asked priests, reverends, teachers, parents, family, and brothers on the corners. All had answers, and all of their answers had some truth, but none completely satisfied me.

Then, I asked my grandmother. She said, "God is good, and all of God's creations have a purpose, all of them." With that answer I felt satisfied and started to formulate my own opinion about good and evil.

It seems that Evil grows in the world of humans as long as Good does nothing. By that I mean, bad people create evil institutions, but these despicable creations grow as long as they are unchallenged. Existence of Evil in this world seems to exist for no other purpose than to challenge Good. Evil makes Good show itself.

Now, for Good to defeat Evil, it must rely on the Creator, and have faith that God stands with the righteous against all odds. If God is with you, who can stand against you?
America, the United States of America, my place of birth, is the greatest challenge to what is good that the world has ever seen. The amount of humans that have been murdered directly or indirectly by my country of birth makes me shake.

From the enslavement of we Africans at the very beginning of the country's history, up to the present, with the CIA selling crack cocaine on every corner of America's cities. I'm sure in the hearts of the founding fathers was good and evil, as all humans have, but evil was the dominating spirit of the founders. They spoke and wrote of good, but practiced evil.

Me, I'm an outlaw in America. I rebel against injustice because I'm trying to get to heaven. I'm not deceived by anything here. I will be free, and gladly die defending it. I believe in GOD and the good that those who believe can do, if they will only try.

I willingly accept my fate as a souljah for the Creator. I must fight however I can. No person of government has authority over me. The land of America is full of tricks that lead to murder. The media with all of its unholy happiness doesn't fool this man. Some will say, "He's so angry."

I counter with, "Why are you so happy?" Is it because your pockets are full of the devil's paper money? Maybe you received awards from Babylon. Maybe the evil you've witnessed hasn't touched one of your loved ones. Maybe you have a "good" job in an evil land. And, if you think America is good, ask yourself, "Why has it killed so many?" And, "Why are so many imprisoned, and so many children hopeless?" For all of America's material wealth, it is completely spiritually poor.

This struggle for freedom consumes me day and night. Some days I feel more optimistic than others. On my optimistic days, I feel as if I can see a better time on the horizon and it uplifts my soul. Other days, optimism seems more like foolishness and I wonder why I am here in this world of sin? It seems at times the world refuses to let me live, and God won't let me die.

I guess this is what slavery is. The longing for more, but having your aspirations become chains to the world of less. Some people are happy here in this world. Not me, and all those like me. You see, I'm a Black Man. My history is full of tragedies. I try to get over it, but I can't.

In my history, the only triumphs are when one of us is honored by one of them. Such contradictions we grow up with. Hearing of slavery and blood; Jim Crow and blood;

segregation and blood; civil rights and blood; and Black Power and blood.

How many in my generation grew up hearing from adults around us how the white man was punishing them, oppressing them, and just out right fucking with them? But every time one of us made it, it was because we had been accepted by them?

I try and reconcile these contradictions in my head, but I fail every time. Sometimes I think if freedom were a person and walked up on me, I would ask him or her what college he or she went to? Or, ask the question: "Who do you work for?"

In this land, you can be whatever you want. Left-Right, Gay-Bi-Straight, Educated-Uneducated, Rich-Poor, whatever you want. The country's government stands for nothing. If you got money, you got power. And, anytime money is power, justice is surely dead.

This world is full of distractions. Anytime the world gets the best of us, we're told to go see a movie, go out to eat, go to the amusement park, visit the nightclub, take a sniff, take a puff, run a line, take a drink, surf the net, or hit some skin.

So here I sit, on a sea-saw in the middle. I don't like either side, left or right. Both sides are full of tricks - forever competing against each other for domination, and forever going up and down.

I'm tired of this. I know it's wrong, so I dream of freedom night and day. The freedom from these contradictions, and to be free of the tricks and deceit.

America said, "In God we trust," yet from the start, it acted as a nation that had no God. Maybe the founding fathers meant they trust that God would forgive them for creating an unholy state.

I say this nation is unholy because it was built by spilling countless amounts of African blood.

We Africans who were kidnapped from our home, and sometimes sold away from home by our own brothers and sisters in Africa, brought to a foreign land, and put in the same class as the farm animals have shed tears from the beginning. But, our tears mixed with our blood meant nothing. It's as if our blood made this beast of a nation thirsty for more.

Have you ever read the stories of Africans who were enslaved and lived to write about it? Their lives were short and they were the victims of constant human brutality. This is what the enslaved Africans said. I ask, "What did we do to these Europeans for them to treat us this way? Then, when I put down the history books and pick up the newspapers of today, I read stories of this nation distributing massive amounts of cocaine in the black neighborhoods of America. I'm talking about the discovery in 1996 that the CIA has controlled all of the drug flow in

America since it's beginning. Then I witness with my own eyes millions of young black males in prison serving sentences for obscene amounts of time for selling drugs.

Now tell me, how does a government manufacture and distribute the drugs, and then prosecute the victim/citizen under its laws? That's the equivalent of me bombing your house, charging you with arson, convicting you, and then placing you in jail for 20 years of your life.

This land of America, brothers and sisters, is a house not at ease. The house is full of dis-eases. The builders of the house thrive in the dis-ease because the dis-ease is no dis-ease to them. It is their creation. Now, this house wants you, the black person, to come in, but it can't tell you its' full of the most unholy disease, the spirit of Satan, the fallen angel, so it must seduce you.

This house is full of things and flesh for pleasure. This house has exotic cars, big screen televisions, lots of clothes and jewels for the body. The builders of this house have technology beyond your imagination. It uses this technology to amplify its seduction of your soul. It created television, radio, computers, movies and telephones to reach you on all sensory levels. Through these machines of idea amplification, it shows you its world of things. It explains to you how the accumulation of another one of its creations, paper money, can give you the ability to have all you see. Now, all of what this house has can be yours. All you need to do is accept its ideas of wealth and it is all yours for the taking.

Let me make it plain, this house I speak of is America. The idea is materialism. Materialism is the worship of material things. When you accept this idea of materialism, you sell your soul to the fallen angel, Satan. Many have sold the most precious gift from the Creator, their soul.

Why do we Africans in America do this? It's as if we've forgotten the past. We forgive a nation for attempted genocide when it has never asked for forgiveness, and acts as if it has done nothing wrong. Which means that it is still attempting genocide.

Can we believe that integration with this house will get us to heaven, when it has done nothing but kill?

I see the corporations as plantations when it concerns we Africans in America. We're treated as less from our entry into the corporation. I believe all the discrimination lawsuits filed proves this point. And just like the plantation, when the whip of the overseer is used unjustly, who do the slaves go to for justice, the plantation owner.

Seeking justice in American courts is stupid. It is the whole government that is conspiring against the Black family. Going to any wing of the house still leaves you in the dis-eased house. If you don't believe me, ask a black person who wins a discrimination case. They win money.

Paper money. Sometimes a little and sometimes a lot. But this isn't a remedy to the problem of unfair treatment, just shut up money. The money is given to shut up the victims, not to prevent future injustices.

Now, many will say that money is power. That's true. But, only for the people that make it. For all those who don't make it, it is a means of control. The paper money keeps our souls in the house that evil built. Ask yourself whose picture is on the money we want? Show me a piece of American paper money that doesn't have the face of a white murderer on it, and you'll be showing me a new currency.

Every time America says it wants to make amends, what does it do? It makes a new law and gives away some more paper money with the original criminals on the money that caused all of this suffering for we Black people in America in the first place.

I plead with you, the reader. You must free yourself from this trickery. Money and laws won't bring back our millions of dead ancestors who met their death during slavery. Money and all the things it can buy amounts to nothing. Don't be deceived by a few Africans in America who have lots of money and things. Make them your leader in life, and you'll find yourself heading to hell in your death.

America is sick from the inside out. It will try and give itself the appearance of a healthy nation. It will talk about its healthy economy.

Every day on the nightly news it tells you how the Dow Jones went up or down. Most of us have nothing to do with the stock market, but we look to it as a barometer of the nations status. The stock market, a market for the exchange of paper, heralds itself as the quickest way to riches. I took money from them, and gave it to charities that try and stop our foresting (that means they try and stop people from cutting down trees). It's just paper.

The television will show countless programs where police officers are the heroes, and citizens are the bad guys. The citizens they attack have broken the law so these programs encourage submission to their authority. But, look around you when you walk outside in your neighborhoods. Police officers are the menace to society.

What you have to remember is that nothing in its right mind, destroys itself. America is no different. It wants to survive. So it seeks to expand itself, to perpetuate itself. It will use all of its assets for its protection. Don't be fooled by political rhetoric.

Everyone has been asking if gangsters go to heaven. I say, yes, if you choose God now. If you're busting shots for street fame and money, for corporate titles, and this Babylon's awards, you're actively choosing hell.

But, here's a chance for you who believe.

If you actively start to challenge this unholy state, you are actively choosing Good, and the Creator is Good.

SHOW BUSINESS

I formally entered show business at the age of 19, but I had literally grown up in the environment. My father was a manager of a sports arena in Kansas City, Missouri. The arena, as all arenas, featured sports and entertainment on a weekly basis, sometimes daily in the summer and fall months.

I got a chance to meet most of my childhood sports heroes because of my father's access. I met Dr. J. I stood side by side with Kareem Abdul-Jabar. I met various other players, and all of them were bigger than life to my young eyes.

Concerts also came to the arena. Although there weren't many acts that I could say were in my age range (this period was in the mid-70's-early 80's before the rap explosion), but I enjoyed the excitement of the concerts. The energy that the arena took on when a popular artist or group was performing was amazing.

I especially enjoyed the backstage action. Here's where I've seen the life of an entertainer take place. I saw lots of beautiful women. All of them assumed I was one of the entertainer's relative since I was most certainly the youngest behind the stage. There were men with sharp suits and lots of gold chains. I thought they looked funny, but they all had a confidence about them, and all had lots of women.

I didn't see much drug use because my father was careful to shield my young eyes from this part of the business. But the alcohol flowed openly, and the air always smelled of marijuana (weed). Everyone had a hustle behind the stage, and everyone looked proud that their hustle had succeeded so well to have gotten them backstage passes.

All of these people behind the stage were my father's friends, and he was theirs. He threw a lot of parties at our house back then. The house would be crawling with the famous and infamous. The driveway and all the neighbors' driveways were filled with the latest model American made cars, and from time to time, a foreign model car.

Mama wasn't the partying type, but tolerated them because my father liked to have his friends around him. They seemed to enjoy his company just as much as he enjoyed theirs.

My father was from Chicago, Illinois, on the "South Side" as he often stated, and brought all of Chicago ways to the Midwest town of Kansas City, Missouri. He drank and smoked, and liked the ladies.

My mother was quite the opposite. She was born and raised in Kansas City, Kansas and didn't like crowds or smoke. She worked at Hallmark Cards, as a lithographic artist, and is still there as of the writing of this book. She works on the "Mahogany" line of cards, which are popular around the country.

My mother and father were complete opposites, but they were married for 14 years, not happily, but together somehow.

Childhood was pretty much a party to me. My father hustled however he could while my mother worked daily. My father believed very much in the Black Power Movement, and his friends reflected his beliefs. They were a mixture of Panthers and Black Muslims, and most of them hustled or had high paying jobs thanks to the opening of society due to the human rights struggle of the 60's and 70's. My mother was with all of this, but her Kansas upbringing kept her as an observer more than a participant.

Now, my first party was in 1987. I was 20 years old and promoted my first party in Kansas City, Missouri at the Westin Crown Center Hotel. How the party came about is a story in itself. I had attended a small state college in Missouri for one year, and then left because I wanted more. The only city I knew of that could hold me was New York City, but I didn't have any money to get there. I had big dreams and knew that I needed money.

Well, I decided that the best way to get money was by throwing a party for profit, but as I stated I didn't have any money.

I thought about getting a loan from my mother, but she despised show business because it had broken up her marriage and family. My father had taken a lost on some sort of venture and didn't have it. So, I went to the one person I knew always kept money and loved me enough to give me money for something so risky, my grand-mother. But, grandma is a businessperson of the magnitude I have yet to meet, and on this day, she schooled me on the subject.

She asked me how much would my party cost. I told her with advertisement, hotel rental, DJ cost, and security, around $1,500. She said she would give me $750. I said, indignantly, "That's not enough, grandma!" She said, "It's enough for me." Then she said, "If you believe in your ideas, you'll find a way." She told me to pray, and sent me on my way. Oh yeah! I didn't have the $750 either. She said she would only give me the $750 when I had the other $750. I told myself, "Damn! This old lady is no joke!" I left wondering how to put this idea in motion.

This first venture taught me something that would help me throughout my life. "The art of transformation." That is, transforming nothing into something. I had nothing but an idea, and nothing to make it more than an idea. Then I realized, I had my mind and the experience of seeing some of the best dealmakers, the backstage hustlers, make an idea into something.

First, I went to the hotel. I spoke with the catering manager and reserved the room for the party. I got a signed contract with both our signatures on it specifying the date and time. The money had to be paid one day before the show.

Second, I took the contract to the local radio station, KPRS, and told them I needed lots of airtime. I spoke with the sales manager who wanted money before he would even produce the ad, let alone play it on the air. This development posed another problem. Once again a great idea, but no money. So, I decided to go directly to the station's owner who was a black man. I felt my idea would make money, and who would better understand the possibility than a black man in business.

I called around for half-day, and then I finally got in touch with the owner's personal assistant. I explained my problem and she was sympathetic. She said to come down the next day. I went and explained my situation. She was an older sister and believed in my idea. She said the owner was out of town, but she would arrange a meeting with the general manager of the station. I told my story to him and he said he liked it, but wondered how I was so sure I could pull this off? I told him I knew lots of people who were in college or working whom wanted to hangout. They were too young for clubs and too old to stay at home.

I told him about the hotel. He knew of it and was surprised I had secured it. Then I told him if he allowed me to help in the production of the ad, it would definitely fly. He asked, "Why is that?"

I said, "You don't play hip-hop, and that' my generations' music. If they hear it, they'll come." The station manager agreed to do it, but had me sign a contract stating that I was responsible for the money owed the station, win or lose. My ads started to run two days later (on a Tuesday), and the party was on a Friday, the 13th. Bad luck to some, good luck to me.

Now, I still didn't have the money. The ads were running and generating a lot of buzz. It was finally the day of the party and I didn't have any money, and the hotel was being swamped with mad calls from young people asking if the party was still on. The hotel management was very nervous. They didn't like the idea of a lot of young people in their recently remodeled hotel.

I had to bring the money to the hotel by 2pm the day of, and it was the day of. I arrived at the hotel at 1:30pm. The catering manager said he no longer was handling my arrangements, but the hotel general manager would be taking over. The general manager was a middle aged Italian, and when he saw my face he looked stunned. He had assumed I was much older. First, he asked if I was in high school. I told him that I had graduated. He then sat down behind his desk and began to explain to me how this party was much bigger than anticipated, and he would need some insurance from me that I could handle this event.

I didn't even have the money for the rental, and now he wanted more money, more security, and possibly for me to take out an insurance policy for the event. And, from what I knew of this business, more security meant more money.

I told him I didn't have the money. He smiled and said, "Our deal is off." Then he got up, escorted me to the door, and closed it behind me.

I had to do something quick. I thought about whom I could get to help me. I realized I needed someone with some weight to vouch for me.

The only person I could think of was a high school friend's father who was a very high city official. We talked many times being that his daughter and I were good friends. We weren't intimate, just friends. We were in the same circle, well I dated some of her girlfriends and we always got along. I called her father at his office. He took my call. I suppose he took it out of curiosity because I had never called him before.

I told him my situation and asked if he could help me. He told me to call him back in thirty minutes. It was 2:30pm. I called him back in thirty minutes. He told me he had spoken with the hotel general manager and the best he could do was get him to listen with an open ear to any plan I had, but he stressed the final decision laid with the Italian general manager of the hotel.

I went back down to the hotel to convince the general manager of my idea. When we sat down again in his office, he looked the same way but didn't act so important. I told him I only had half the money for the rental. Then, I explained to him how I knew the money would be made on the door. He said I couldn't possibly guarantee a success.

Then I told him, I couldn't, but the way his switchboard had been lighting up, the party was already a success. He was still listening. I said, I would give the hotel $500 more dollars. He said, "What about the crowd control." He wanted more security and he wanted the added security to be off duty policemen. Off duty policemen wanted $15 per hour. The party was 4 hours, and he wanted five of them. That was another $300. That brought the total to $2,300. I told him I would give him $750, which was the agreed upon rental fee, and the other $1,350 by midnight. He agreed, but said the police had to be on the premises before the door opened, and he would shut the party down if the $1,350 wasn't in his hands by midnight. I agreed, and then signed another contract, which his secretary typed in fifteen minutes. I had the room. I then told the general manager I would give him the $750 in two hours. He said, "Two hours, or no go." I said, "I'll be back in two hours. It was 3:30pm.

My grandmother lived close to the hotel. I went to her house and explained what I had done, then asked if she could give me the money. Now Grandma, being a top-flight businessperson, wanted to take the money to the general manager personally. I tried to talk her out of it, but she said she had to see the man's face. So we drove to the hotel, Grandma and I. We entered the general manager's office, and he looked confused. I looked ashamed. I thought I was a big business man, and my grandmother comes with me to close my first deal.

She spoke to the general manager, and to my surprise, they hit it off. Grandma thanked him for taking a risk on her grandson. She said I was trustworthy and would make good on my deal. She gave him the money. We left at 5:45pm.

I took grandma home, and then she asked me when the set started. I told her 10pm, and she said she would be there at 9:30pm. I said, "What?" She said she wanted the first $750. I said, "What? Again?" She explained, "You're my grandson and I'm your grandmother. We're family, and family comes before everyone except God." She said, "The general manager is nice, but he ain't God."

I understood and never forgot that point. I left at 6:15pm. Still hadn't secured the police, so I called the police department and asked for five off duty policemen. They said it was short notice, but that another party had cancelled just an hour earlier, my competition. The night was looking good, I thought.

The policemen wouldn't get paid until the end of the night I told her. She said that it was standard procedure that they get half up front and the other at the end. I told her that I could only pay them at the end of the night. She paused, and then said ok.

It was 7pm. I took a shower, got dressed, and called the DJ to see if he needed any help. He said he was cool. I called my partners who were going to help at the door, and wherever else needed.

My brother Maurice and I left the house around 8pm to go pick everybody up. We arrived at the hotel at 8:30pm. The DJ pulled up at the same time. We hauled in everything, and set the room up for a party. I left to pick up grandma. We got back at 9:30pm. To my surprise, there was literally a traffic jam in front of the hotel. Brothers and sisters were out in full force. We went to the ballroom and opened the doors at 10pm sharp. The police arrived while I was out picking up grandma.

Grandma sat right behind the money collector, my brother, and I watched every dollar. I gave her $750 at 10:30pm, and gave the general manager his $1,350 at 11pm. At the end of the night, I had admitted 1250 people at $5 per person. My first gig was a success to say the least. I made $6,250 (minus expenses, I made $3,950).

I was in show business, and headed for New York City. This was how I entered show business. It was fun, and the money was good. There were a lot of perks being a promoter. There were always women around, and popularity was mandatory. I was the man in my world.

I stopped doing parties when I turned 21. It got sort of boring. I was doing parties all over the country by this time, and had met quite a few industry people nationwide, and wanted to advance. I was living in Harlem at the time. Well, I maintained an apartment, although I kept my home private. I'm like my mother in this.
My home is private. At this time, I traveled a lot, and made a lot of money. I had friends all over the nation it seemed. But, I especially liked Washington, D.C.

I liked Howard University, and had been accepted to attend Howard when I graduated High School. I even went so far as to register for classes. I had an average high school GPA, but I had great SAT scores. I never attended any classes though. Business called, and D.C. was a prime spot for throwing parties because it had lots of young black people and plenty of clubs - a promoter's dream.

I threw quite a few parties in D.C. at this time. It was 1987 and the business was opening up to young blacks thanks to the rise of hip-hop. I met lots of young energetic people at Howard

University, and at my D.C. parties. Some were brilliant, I must say. A few stayed in show business and became main players in the show business industry. But, I met them all at my parties, and all of them fascinated me.

At this time, I also became acquainted with a well-known television star from a very popular show. We met in D.C. and became fast friends. We had a lot of the same interest - money, clothes, and women. He was famous, while I was behind the scenes. Never did I use my name promoting parties, and my circle of friends was small, tight, and outside of my own parties. From time to time, I went to clubs to check out the competition, and I never went to large gatherings of people on the regular.

The television star and me kicked it though. I liked the access he had to America. Wherever we went, people knew him - black and white. They seemed to love him. Girls mobbed him at malls and me too, because I was with him.

He stopped appearing on the show and moved to D.C. to attend Howard University. This was even better for me; my best friend was where I made the most money. And, we both loved Harlem. He was born there, and I was a transplant. We traveled a lot.

I still did parties, but as stated before, I wanted to advance. So, I started doing concerts. The first concert I did was with an upcoming female R&B singer who had a hot single on the radio. I quickly found out concerts were more complicated than parties, mostly because of the star factor.

I discovered the fans are finicky about who they come see perform. It's a very personal thing. Plus the ticket prices are higher, and the concert atmosphere is more charged than a party. After all, a star is in the house.

The first concert I promoted was in Kansas City, Missouri where I started all this. My partner, the television star, went with me and we stayed at my mother's house. My mother was glad to see us, as usual, and the mid-western city of Kansas City, Missouri was very happy to see the television star in person. Although we had visited before, this time we were promoting. Rather, I was promoting, and where I went, he went too. We had fun, but as I said earlier, concerts are different from parties.

I did everything wrong, but the booking agent in New York was a friend and he helped me cover my mistakes which were plentiful.

The day of the concert arrived and the star arrived that morning. She and her entourage were extremely difficult. They wanted the most expensive of everything. I would run into this problem over and over again in concert promotion. The stars and their entourage assumed because I was so young to be doing this that I had to be a drug dealer. Where else would I get the cash for this type of business?

They found out though, that it was through conservative spending, not from throwing bricks (kilos of cocaine) on the street.

Well, my first show was a complete failure. I lost all the money I had invested. The concert was lightly attended, and the star and her entourage ran up an outrageous hotel tab. I lost, and couldn't stand it. I went back to New York in a miserable mood.

My friend, the agent, was cool though. He gave me shows in bigger markets with more established artists. I was becoming a sensation in the business side of show business, and enjoyed my status, but something was wrong.

As I mentioned, I traveled a lot. When I went to cities to promote concerts, I met lots of people. I also saw lots of neighborhoods. I started to notice that we Africans in America were turning our neighborhoods into something different from what I remembered in my younger days.

The neighborhoods were increasingly violent, and my concerts were reflecting the increase.

It started what seemed like overnight, but it had started. Every concert ended in violence or stopped prematurely because of violence. I saw fights at concerts and parties when I was young, and at my own functions.

I even heard the occasional bust of a 22 handgun in the parking lot. Usually the owner was aiming the gun in the air, and rarely did I see one leveled at a human, but this changed.

Public Enemies' message of Black Unity seemed to be hitting hard, but from my unique view of the society, I could see it was all window dressing. People were definitely feeling the pain that Public Enemy and many others were rapping and singing about, but they weren't analyzing their pain. They were desperately trying to escape the pain.

I started seeing lots of high price clothes on the concert's attendees. The cars were flashy and the parking lot brawls became mini wars with high-tech automatic gunfire, the choice weapon now. Gone were the 22s, 9mms were becoming trendy. My concerts were no longer sources of entertainment, they became places where hustling rivals met and had it out. The women seemed to be reflecting this new lifestyle too. The backstage action was becoming scandalous, even to my eyes, which grew up in this thing called show business. They had a look of desperation in their eyes, as if they could end their day to day struggle if they could make a hustler fall in love with them, or at least like the sex enough to pay the rent.

I spoke to many of these sisters during this period of my life. They changed my view of the world I lived in. They wore tight and short skirts, and had beautiful bodies to show off. Their light brown to dark black skin was flawless. Their fingernails and toe nails, immaculate. Their hair was Did! The sisters appeared to have it all together, but conversation beyond sex and entertainment revealed so much more. Most of these young Queens had children and were raising them alone. They worked in an office, or were on some sort of government assistance. Most worked, and the ones that didn't, were trying and wanted more.

I discovered the impact of videos. I had been on lots of video sets before this, and had developed a love for the motion picture camera. I liked the making of videos, and all the excitement. But, I had no idea how powerful the messages of sex and material fulfillment by all means necessary were doing to the young black mind - male and female.

These sisters told me all types of stories about their lives. Up until this time, I had never listened to women. I had female friends and a few girlfriends, but never had I engaged them about their dreams. I just assumed they all wanted a big house and lots of money. Although some ladies wanted this, and would do anything to get it, they were not the norm. They were the exception. Overwhelmingly the sisters were worried about their neighborhood and what kind of world their children were being raised in.

I discovered that lots of their brothers and boyfriends were in prison. Life was hard for these sisters, but they carried on. The brothers I met wanted money. They believed money was freedom and power, and were willing to risk their young lives in pursuit of it. I admired their spirit but rejected their vehicle for success, which was hustling drugs. Every city I went to, I met these brothers first. In their cities, they were Princes. They had the connects and people feared them. I spent many nights talking with these brothers. We talked about business and life, mine and theirs.

They were fascinated with my life, and I, by theirs. These brothers taught me the street game of the 90's, drug dealing, and I taught them about show business, and all it's potential, if we young black males could organize ourselves. But, mostly they liked the money and women idea of it all. I never ventured into drugs, but many of them ventured into show business.

Imagine my surprise when some of the brothers I had turned on to concert promotion were now competition with me for shows, and had more money than I did to spend on an act.

I traveled alone a lot, and had my own hotel room. It was always the same hotel as the acts I was promoting. After the show, I went to my room, calculated my profits, sometimes losses.

I called my mother, brother, father and grandmother. Later, I would call a few friends, and then I would just sit in the room ignoring the phone ringing and the women knocking on my door for sex, and the brothers trying to get put on in the business. As you can see, my profile was low, very low, and my enthusiasm for show business was just as low. About this time, I wanted to get out of the concert business. I began to have experiences with friends and money that were turning my usual trust into doubt. As the late 80's music scene exploded, the stakes got higher. Rap music was selling like crack, and both were making millionaires out of a few top flight players in the game.

I decided to finally leave the concert business when my friend, the television star, turned on me for money.

Concert negotiations were of an increasingly complex nature, so I decided to hire a black entertainment lawyer to handle my small but growing business. To my surprise, I found an all black law firm in Washington, D.C. and most of the lawyers had attended Howard University. They had my trust from the start, and decided to hire them for my first concert outside of the country. I had planned a concert on the island of St. Thomas/Virgin Islands. It was a hip-hop show that I hoped would be well attended on the Caribbean Island.

These attorneys didn't know much about the nuts and bolts of show business, I discovered, and had little or no contacts in the industry. But, they knew the contractual law of America, and show business is a contract driven industry. Contracts are made and broken at a furious pace in show business, and for this reason, I stayed with them.

They told me since I didn't have an office of my own (I worked out of my apartment in Harlem), that I could use their office. I accepted their offer. During the planning and implementation of a concert requires lots of phone calls, even more faxes, and a couple of visits to the city where the concert is to be held. Maybe more, depending on the size of the show. Well, I made all these phone calls with the lawyers present because I wanted to introduce my contacts and friends to them, plus I liked the idea of putting people on the speakerphone and saying my lawyer is present. I had a big head, and they encouraged its growth. A month went by and the lawyers knew all of my contacts and had picked my brain with question after question about the business, in particular, the rap industry.

One day I came into the office after a trip home to New York. They informed me the deal has been changed. They had called the agents without my knowledge and changed the contracts. The changes were that they, the law firm, was now the promoter of record and I was simply an investor. This change meant they could decide on my cut, and if I didn't agree, they could kick me out the deal. They did this because of my big head. I had literally given them power over my business affairs because I constantly introduced them as my attorneys, and used their office to work out of. Why would anyone doubt that the requested changes weren't from me, no matter how absurd?

They told the agents and the act's managers that the changes were being made because of tax reasons. Everyone in show business knows about taxes, and I'm sure understood. Now, of course my share of the potential profits was now half, and that's if I put up all the money. If I refused, they would put up the money and give me nothing.

I refused and lost my show, but as I said earlier, I lost a friend, a good friend, in a fucked up deal. See, the television star was also part of the deal. Sometimes I would pay him to host a show. He needed the money, and more importantly, we were friends. I would've given him the money even if he didn't host a show, but he said it was a good way to "keep his face out there." I agreed.

This show in the Caribbean was my biggest, and I wasn't going to leave him out, so I made him the host and lined up several local appearances for him on the island to promote the show and his career. We agreed $3,000 plus all expenses. I assumed once he found out about what had happened, he would refuse to host. They offered him more money, a better hotel, and he accepted.

This shocked me because we were friends, and that meant more than money to me, but not to him.

I was hurt by this, but still believed in friendship, and this belief has always been the basis of my life. I said I would never accept this world's "friend today, enemy tomorrow" philosophy, but I would learn in the future that this is a reality in this world of sin.

I went back to New York and took up other interest. One was filmmaking, and the other, computer technology. It was now late 1990, and I had gotten a loft apartment in the village on Sullivan Street. I got the place because I liked the artsy scene, and the village was, and is, one of the most unique places to live in the world. I still had the place uptown (Harlem), but the village was where I lived mostly.

I hung out on film sets, took classes on film at a local university in the morning, visited sets of movies and videos in the afternoon, read about computers in the evening, and partied the rest of the night. I got on the sets of films and videos because of my concert promotion status. I met lots of people during those years and stayed in contact with most.

I learned a lot by watching films and videos being made. I started to see filmmaking as a vehicle for getting an idea to a lot of people. I had no idea what I wanted to present, but I loved the movies.

I watched mad films during this time. I had always watched films, but I watched them with a different eye now that I understood the process of making one.

I was blown away by the Japanese filmmaker, Akiro Kurosawa. His breathtaking films got me wondering how films could be used to express an idea, but in a very dramatic way by using cinematography and locations. I like Spike Lee, too. His films had a reality base to them. I could write volumes about my love of films, but this isn't the place for it.

I also took an interest in computers and the upcoming computer technology. I found computers fascinating. They taught me a lot about this world we live in. I say this because I saw the world becoming more dependent on computer technology, and I wanted to know about the possibilities of these machines. I discovered that most of the banking systems were run by computer technology. I used computer technology in banking and didn't even realize the simplicity of it, and the scam of it.

During this period, I lived a lot like my father did. I had lots of parties in my loft, and lots of girlfriends. I was 23 years old.

TELEVISION

I've watched television for as long as I can remember. Throughout my childhood it was a source of entertainment and information. The television helped in shaping my values, along with my parents, teachers, clergymen, and adult family members.

On the surface, this sounds like a healthy balance for a young man, but when I go deeper than appearances, I see the real impact of this thing called television. This T.V. gave me a healthy dose of some hidden person or person's ideology, and unknowingly me and millions of other children accepted it wholeheartedly. Even when the television presented a life that demeaned my own existence.

I remember the fascination my family had with "Dallas" and "Dynasty." Two night time soap operas that chronicled the lifestyles of the rich and famous. We loved it, even though our lifestyle could've been called, "lifestyles of the barely making it and anonymous." As I watched such shows, little did I know that these shows, and countless others were shaping what I expected from life. Which to state plainly, I grew up wanting to be "RICH."

As I grew older, the television matured with me. I loved rap music and still do. But, television turned my love and respect for the only original ghetto art form of my lifetime into a fascination. The videos started to reflect my aspirations and desire much more so than regular television programming. Who didn't get excited when you first saw Public Enemy's "Fight the Power" video? This video is an excellent example of what I'm writing about.

As I stated earlier, I grew up wanting a lifestyle that was beyond my reach, and I became frustrated. Public Enemy and groups on the same vibe were educating me and a generation to why we had less, and through the videos, started to visually simulate what I felt like doing. I loved it, and anticipated every new video from these type of artists. They were true revolutionaries in my eyes.

The only problem was that I escaped reality, and vented my anger through this thing called television. I'm sure that a great many of these artists truly believed they were sparking a full blown revolution among our generation, but I felt I didn't have to really do it in the real physical world. I just let it be known to the world that I agreed with these artists, and bumped Pubic Enemy as loud as my 75 Ford Maverick could take. Still, I never did what I so loved watching – open rebellion for positive action.

As you know, this period of rap was short lived. I still hadn't conquered my desire for riches. I just became more determine because my childhood images of wealth and luxury seemed the way to end the misery of all us "have nots." As usual, the television sent me images to reinforce this misplaced feeling, but not the images of the rap/revolutionaries, which were new to me, and ran completely counter to what I had been told was the way to get rich.

These images of material things hit at the deepest part of me, my childhood. All of a sudden, images of hoes, clothes and bankrolls flooded my television, and I watched and longed to have it all.

The images of revolution were pulling me away from this world of sin, yet these images of material things were pulling me into the center of the Americans machine of oppression, "Lust for material things." It's worked on every generation since this country's founding, and didn't miss mine, the 20 something.

Some of us got deep into the drug game, which provided instant riches. But, this game was and is more than a game. Some of my brothers and sisters got rich, but our whole race paid a price that is incalculable. Our whole generation became introduced to urban warfare. Not the revolutionary kind where young men and women organize themselves to resist those that would enslave them. This urban warfare was materially motivated. It was about clothes, hoes and bankrolls, and the greatest victims were young black males and females.

We're now suffering the aftermath of the drug game in unholy numbers. Many of my generation and the generation behind ours are suffering under incredibly long prison sentences. Not only is the individual hurt, but irreparable damage is caused to the parentless children who are the wish, in flesh, of our generation.

Drug addiction, once again, not only harms the individual, but also crushes the family of the addict, and humiliates the community that is the environment of a drug addict. The drug war was, and is, a War on Young Black People, and our future families. Negative images of young Black males flooded the T.V. They became, and still are, the profile of a criminal. But, in spite of all of this, the drug game flourished and began to dominate the videos. Hustlers and gangsters were the thing to be.

Let me state at this point, I'm not against hustlers and gangsters. I feel you, and know why you're in the game. But, I'm writing to tell you the game is a trap designed before we were born.

I know you want more. I know it's hard to make ends meet. But, brothers, we got to raise up out of this cycle of jail, drugs and death.

I'm not saying that retreating to the white man's world is a way of advancing. I'm telling you to get bolder. I'm asking you to turn the television off, and your mind on. The television is bullshit. We need real action, NOW! What we need is a new nation - a nation that serves our interest. Our generation can, and must, break this cycle of clothes, hoes and bankrolls.

We don't make the clothes. Our women are much more than whores. Money ain't nothing but paper with green pictures of dead white men who shitted on us when they were alive. We deserve and need more!

JAIL

Jail was a place I was raised to fear, and at all cost avoid. All the adults told me that jail was a place for criminals, enemies of the state. Yet, all my heroes in my childhood had been in jail. The most influential convict I admired was Jesus the Christ.

My young heart loved Jesus. Reading the Bible was a magical experience for me. I loved every parable of his. For my sixth grade religion class, I memorized the "Temptation of Christ" - when Jesus is in the desert, and Satan takes him to the mountaintop offering him the world if he will only bow down and worship the Devil. Jesus resisted temptation, and I cheered him on. It made no difference to me that I was almost 2,000 years removed from this episode. I believed in Jesus' strength.

I was raised Catholic. I went to Catholic schools from the third grade all the way to my high school graduation. I adored Christ.
I worshipped Christ. I believed. But, Jesus was a criminal to the Romans and Jewish people of his day. He was indicted, tried, convicted, and sentenced to death. Jesus was an outlaw.

You see, I was raised to be under the influence of Christ at all times. My mama is the cause of this mostly, and I give her my eternal thank you for this. However, years later, Mama and I started to see things different.

The world I was maturing in, the world I lived in, seemed to be the same world Christ lived in. Nothing had changed much to me. The faces had changed, names had changed, but still the righteous were persecuted, and the deceitful praised.

Yet, I was raised to believe in Christ, and believe I did. Yet, believing didn't seem to be enough for me. I believed, but nothing changed. So, I decided to start living my beliefs and, here is where my life took a drastically different course than the one I was raised to follow.

I embraced Jesus' life wholly, therefore, I consciously chose the way of an outlaw in this life. My first act was to take from the rich and give to the poor. It was a simple conclusion to me. This world was wicked to me so, being a newly initiated soul-jah, I took their money.

I took money from a rich corporation, and gave it back to the poor people who I believed they stole it from. They were too slow in divesting in South Africa, so I helped them speed it up. I took $150,000, gave $120,000 away to charities and individual victims of the American Holocaust – Slavery (which continues to this very day).

I invested $25,000 in businesses. I didn't have any ownership in any of them, but my friends who I lent money to, got introduced to redlining.

Let me explain this concept of Redlining for all who've never heard of it. Redlining is when banks decide that a particular part of a city is undesirable for investment. That means, if you walk into a bank with great credit, and want a loan to start a business or buy a house in a neighborhood that falls within a redlined zone, you will be turned down automatically. You'll be given an excuse, but in the end, you got nothing. Redlining is one way that keeps poor communities, poor. 99.9% of the time, wherever there is a high concentration of Black souls in a city, the banks in that city redline it.

Well, I contributed to those I believed were good people, and wanted to do some good for the hood. And, low and behold, after I gave my last ghetto grant, I got a knock on my door from three FBI agents. My charge was for wire fraud, and of course I was convicted.

Wire fraud means I used electronic equipment and telephones (wire) to commit fraud, hence wire fraud. You're probably wondering how I did it, but this book is about freedom, not about paper money, one of the greatest tools against freedom.

Even though I consciously and willingly had broken the law, I went to trial to prove that I was innocent. Although my actions were firm and decisive, my mind was soft and timid. The lawyer I had, argued law. I knew he should have argued righteousness. I was right, I believed. The law was protecting the rich and preying on the poor. Attack the greed of the few I told him. He said I was naïve. He argued law. After a hung jury, and a retrial, I was found guilty. They convicted me for my actions, but I knew my cause was righteous. I was following the way of Christ. I was sentenced to 29 months in federal prison. I was 23 years old.

I served 25 months in Allenwood Federal Prison Camp. My crime was white-collar. Throughout all of this, I stayed the course. I was determined to follow in Jesus' footsteps. Black or white, I was going to follow Christ. I was raised this way.

In Allenwood, I didn't go to church. I had stopped going to church when I was 16 years old. The church was not satisfying to me, but Jesus and his father, God, were more than enough for me. The scriptures were always at the forefront of my thoughts. The words and deeds of Christ were a beacon of light for me.

My time in jail was a time of learning. I read lots of books and had long conversations with some of America's most infamous criminals.

I met many different men, good and bad, but all real. To give you some idea of the type of men I met and conversed with, I'll tell you about my first cellmate (my cellie). He had been a Federal Court Judge in a large northeastern city, and was convicted of accepting bribes. He confirmed my belief that the American Judicial System was corrupt.

Now one may say, "What do you mean, Kheop? The system worked, it caught a dirty judge on the take." You see, he wasn't brought to justice because he took bribes; he was brought to justice because he refused to take bribes. Now, in the U.S. Federal Courts, an honorable, God fearing man is highly unpopular. I'm glad to say, this Judge was a Black man.

In jail, I met lots of brothers who were doing unholy amounts of time for selling drugs. Even then, most of them were telling me the government was the real drug dealer. This was in 1992. In the fall of 1996, it was uncovered that the CIA was, and is, behind all illegal cocaine powder and rock in America.

The more I read about the lives of men and women who had chosen Christ, the firmer I became in the life, the outlaw life. Reading about ancient Africa, Egypt in particular, was uplifting to a young brother. Knowing from reading the Bible that Jesus had been brought into Egypt for safety because of his outlaw status even as an infant, made learning about Egypt more exciting. I learned a lot of facts about Egypt and Africa, the continent that it is a part of. I became introduced to Islam - the Nation of Islam. Reading about Elijah Muhammad, and seeing young and old brothers in prison with me still vibing and believing in the truth he brought, was amazing.

At this time, I read the Quran. I was moved deeply by the life of Prophet Muhammad. The book he was inspired to write, the Quran, was spiritual, lyrical, outlaw poetry. It touched my soul the way reading about Jesus Christ had done when I was a child in Kansas City, Missouri sitting in my father's chair on a cold winter night with the fire going and reading about the temptation of Christ.

I felt Prophet Muhammad deeply.

To me, the Quran was somewhat similar to the Bible. Jesus is mentioned many times. All the prophets of the Bible are respected in the Quran.

Here I was in a federal prison, in the mountains of Pennsylvania, having the same feeling. I knew then that I had chosen correctly for me, but still, I had to travel much further. The Quran elevated my belief. I started to see that Jesus was a man who had chosen to believe in God. Not the God in the sky, but the God in him.

I understood that his battles were not with the world, but with himself. He was his father. He knew he was God, but saying it isn't enough. He had to live the life of God. Muhammad was the same way. He lived the word of God. He saw no conflict in using the sword and practicing the holy words of God (Allah).

Jesus manifested God for his times, and Muhammad, his times. I started to see something that was bigger than the flesh. Something bigger than time itself. Throughout history I could see that many men and women had chosen the way of Jesus and Muhammad long before either was born to this world. The way had been well established and written about. I was clearly traveling, but I was in jail, and the time went slow at times, and fast other times.

I eventually was released with three years of supervised release. Supervised Release is the federal form of probation. I caught my case in Washington, D.C., so I had to return to D.C. I was assigned a federal probation officer, and I was introduced to jail outside of jail. My probation officer (p.o.) told me she was here to help me, but I told her I had done my time and needed no assistance from her. I told her this in a nice way, but there really isn't a nice way to disagree with a government official. We were not friends.

As I said earlier, I was firmly on the path. I saw the probation officer as an intrusion, an obstacle. She was a representative of what I believe to be the cause of all the nations problems. I went to jail because I disagreed with the law. Now the law wanted me to live in accordance with it. I disagreed when I broke the law two years earlier, and nothing had changed my beliefs. Prison and studying made me firmer in my resistance to government authority.

I wanted to leave D.C. and go back to Harlem, but my probation officer said, "No." I didn't have freedom to move anymore. I decided to move anyway, and decided not to tell the p.o.

I went back to Harlem, and was living my life for almost a year. Then one morning around 6am, I hear a knock at the door. My roommate answered the door. It was the U.S. Marshals. Like a coward, and very unChrist like, I tried to hide in a closet. The marshals found me and arrested me. They took me to the Federal Metropolitan Corrections Center, better known as MCC.

I went to court, and the judge had the marshals take me back to D.C. The same judge who sat on the bench during my trial, was the judge I had to go back in front of. Needless to say, he removed me from supervised release and sentenced me to 10 months in prison for violating my probation. He also said after the 10 months, I no longer had to be on supervised release. So, off I went to Schukyll Federal Prison Camp for 10 months. I was pissed off, and somewhat ashamed at being back in prison. I hadn't even been out a full year, and here I was back in prison again.

My mother was devastated. My grandmother almost didn't accept my collect calls, but she did. Thank you Grandma. I tried to explain to my mother why I had chosen to break the rules of supervised release, but still I could hear the pain in my mama's voice. Once I got over the daze of being in prison again, I set about to continuing my travels of the mind.

I read books, but books didn't hold my attention this time. I started to talk more with the brothers around me. I wasn't just talking, I was listening to them. We were from different cities, but we were all traveling at this time.

When I was at Allenwood Federal Prison, I met an older brother. He had been a founding member of a very, very popular 60's and 70's R&B group on Motown Records. We were friends from our first conversation. He told me all about America through his eyes. His stories and conversations were like water to a man who had been lost in the desert. He told me all about the record business. He gave me a first hand account of Motown Records. He had traveled the world several times, but was still a down to earth brother from Detroit. He had much love for all we young brothers, and gave his time and knowledge to all of us, me in particular.

It was because I grew up in show business and knew some of his old show business friends. He even knew the general manager of the Kansas City radio station who took a chance on me when I promoted my first party.

I learned about the great Black entertainers that only someone like him could teach. He never gossiped, and never blamed anybody for his situation. He was a man about his. He even wrote a few songs while I was there. One thing I remember him teaching me was to rely on myself. He explained how he wrote music, and why he wrote music. He said it was all belief in the goodness of his heart, the goodness of God. The business had made him weary, but the music will be forever in his heart.

Now in Schukyll, I spoke and hung out more with guys my own age. It was where I met a Latino brother, Carlos, but he prefers to be called Carlito or Cee. He and I became friends because of my looking for conversation. Cee was really into Hip-Hop. I was too, we all were, but Cee was Hip-Hop. He loved the music and the culture it produced. He had all these Source magazines on his desk in his cube (sleeping area). One day I asked to see one, and we've been friends ever since. Cee and I talked for hours about any and everything. He told me about his life, and I spoke about mine. But our common passion was the truth.

Cee was also a writer. He showed me some of the pieces he wrote, and I was thoroughly impressed. He was the first person my age that showed me that a person could express how they feel on paper.

There was a brother who was the youngest on the compound, Eloheim. He was 19 when he came to the feds. He was serving a five-year bid, and was older in his mind than he was in years. He, Cee and myself were friends, and we still are to this very day. Both of them are in

New York where I am, and both are forever my brothers.

At this time I gained a greater understanding of Islam because of Cee. He was studying Islam intensely. He followed the Islamic path truly. I had even more respect for Islam when Cee told me the hard path he had traveled, and how Islam had given him light when he most needed it. I was still searching, and believed in the lives of Jesus and Muhammad, yet, I knew there was more. The holy books told of the failures and triumphs of the human soul. They told of the miraculous deeds that can be achieved when belief transforms into doing. When I looked at the world I lived in, I knew this is a world in need of a miracle.

I got released in the spring of 1994. I went back to Harlem for a little while and traveled to Atlanta, Georgia. I was considering attending Morehouse College, but I decided to go back to Howard University in D.C.

After all my time in jail, almost three years, I respected education in a way I didn't before. I was 27 years old when school started in the fall of 1994. I told people I was 24 because I didn't want to explain prison. I was at college and I simply wanted to move on, but there can be no advancing for me, or anyone, in life until peace is made with the past.

I went to class everyday. I made the Deans List my first semester back, but during the spring semester, I became bored. I began talking to other students about the problems of our time. I wanted to do something – wanted to take action. I felt as if I was abandoning the life of an outlaw. I felt myself getting comfortable, yet I knew this wasn't the time to rest. I just needed a break. Well, I had my break and wanted some action.

I decided to start a business. I needed money and didn't want to rob the rich anymore. I had discovered that even rich people are struggling to survive in this world. Not materially, but spiritually. Still, I had tuition and rent to pay. So, along with a friend, I started a shuttle bus for other students. This venture did financially well for us. Then I decided to create a café along with some friends. I believed that if we made some money, we could pay the bills and use the excess to help the community. It was simple to me and I wondered why I hadn't done this before.

Once the café was open, it was doing well. It was a place of meeting for various groups and students. Professional and political groups met there. Children from the neighborhood came in after school, and I was glad that we could pay them a few bucks to help around the café. People of all colors and class were frequenting the café. It was a success. Yet, even with the café, I was still restless. Business didn't provide the peace of mind I thought it would. Some people want to make an impact or a contribution to the world, and this is cool with me. I wanted to change the world.

At this time, I was seriously studying Islam, and becoming vaguely aware of my own spirituality. I was starting to feel my own divinity. No longer was I content to worship great men and women. I wanted to become great. I wanted to live this life to it's fullest. I wanted righteousness to be my legacy. School was low on my list of priorities, but learning was my top priority. Howard University is a good school, but I no longer desired the classroom setting. I wanted to live it.

I had read so much about injustices in America, and throughout the world, that I despised racism and all its many characteristics. Police brutality bothered me in a deeply spiritual way. All police aren't bad, but the ones that are overshadow the good ones. The institution of a police force seems to breed schoolyard bullies gone drunk on power. As I became somewhat successful as a café owner, the success attracted jealous and envious people.

The worse kind of jealousy is official jealousy. You know the kind of jealousy that if a young Black man has a decent car, he is profiled as an enemy of the nation. When we drive Black and thugged out, we're not American citizens enjoying our lives, pursuing what makes us happy. We are Niggas, Hated Niggas, and Despised Niggas. Some police assume they are doing the nation a favor by harassing us every chance they get.

I know some brothers are up to no good, but so are the white males in Mercedes. So are the Generals in uniform. So are the white males in corporate America. Yet, only we are seen as criminals. I've heard it said before by a so-called respected scientist, that we Black people are born criminals. If this is so, then all white male babies are born mass murderers since white males are the general and overwhelming mass murderer. All they say is, "God made me do it" and all is understood and forgiven. War upon war, countless civilizations destroyed by jealous and envious white males and females.

I was told many times, and in as many different ways, that I should forgive them. I should pray for them. That we Black people should stop crying and move on. But, if I or any other young brother, or sister, drive a nice car, a machine, we are criminals.

Some white scientist says we are born criminals. I guess they've forgotten about all the wars we Black men and women fought for "our" country. But, I'll move on.

As the café grew, certain police got hot for me, in particular. Certain police harassed customers if they parked in the "legal" parking in front of the café. Countless tickets and numerous dirty looks were received.

Now, here I am, 29 years of age. I've been a soul-jah for years, and yet I still feel afraid of police and the guns they carry. This is when I started to leave the books and something else started to grow. It was a fire that was growing in me, and the flame wanted to escape. I started meditating and praying about this fire, this feeling inside. I needed some understanding. No one had answers. I started to see that this was something I had to go through alone.

My spirit became determined. I felt myself headed for a battle, but didn't know who I was to battle. I was telling myself that the next time a police interferes with my life, I would not cooperate. I refused in my own heart to submit to anyone or any institutions' authority. I was enlightened enough to know when I was a victim of injustice, and decided it was time to resist. Then the question arose in me. "How? And, with what?" I did not want to kill a police officer, any citizen, or anything, and I was raised to believe in Jesus. Belief was not enough. I had to start doing.

TO THE POLICE

What's up, Mr. and Ms. Police Officer, Federal Agent, Undercover, and all who support the police and military in America?

First, let me introduce myself. My name is Michael Kheop. I was born and raised in America like most of you. I went to high school and then to college. And, the million-dollar question is, what's my race? African, still in America - a Black man. And, oh yeah, I'm an Outlaw until I free this land, or you kill me.

Let me explain why I chose this life of an Outlaw. Here in America, we have laws and courts that decide what is just and unjust. Who gets punished and who doesn't. This justice system as all justice systems in the world is the backbone of the nation, and claim to be blind to race, color, religion, and social economic class.

Now, all human institutions are corruptible because some humans are corrupt. Not all humans are corrupt, not all institutions are corrupt, but history proves, left unchecked these human created institutions become predators of humans.

America is in such a position. Corruption of the moral and economic leadership in this country is of such a great proportion that good deeds are the aberration, and bad deeds are the norm.

I grew up in America. I've seen scandal after scandal. I see schools being closed and prison construction being accelerated. I see you, the law enforcement community, as the front lines of the war between God's will and the Devil's deceit.

Yes, I mentioned God in connection with law enforcement. I do this because the Creator of all is the only true law enforcer. You are not a law enforcement official because you were not deputized by God. You could never enforce God's laws, but you're fully capable of enforcing human laws.

Now, the human laws you enforce are unjust to me, so it's no law at all in my eyes. This may sound as if I disrespect the law. I don't disrespect laws that are in harmony with God's laws, but if I see that they're not, I have a human right to rebel against these laws. Remember, America was founded by people who felt that the laws that governed them were unjust, so they exerted their most basic human right, the right to resist unjust laws.

You see, I don't consider myself a tough guy or a bad ass. I just believe in freedom more than I fear you. A lot of you law enforcement officials follow the orders that are given to you by humans, but rebel against God's orders. I can't possibly tell you what God's will is, but the foundation, I believe, is good.

You law enforcement officials are enforcing laws that are not good. You know as well as me that the war on drugs never stopped the flow of illegal drugs. You know prisons don't prevent crime. Yet, you are the main component in the war against drugs, and you bring the captured human souls to the prisons that evil built.

You say it's just your job. But, when does your job stop, and love consciousness begin? Remember, these are humans you incarcerate, and sometimes kill. Do you believe your souls won't be judged when you die? You, like all we humans, have one final journey to make after your death, and your life will speak for you, not your mouth, not medals, awards and commendations from your superiors. Your life will speak for you. And, if the laws you enforce don't solve the problem of why they were created, and you know better than anyone if a law is working, and you still enforce the law, you in fact are breaking the law.

Now, some of you don't believe in this political, religious, supernatural talk. You believe in your paycheck. The paycheck that feeds, clothes, and shelters your family. But, your paycheck comes attached with all the blood you have spilled, families you've broken, and souls you've condemned to hell on earth. You say you can see your superiors and your paycheck, and this God I speak of is not here. Let me ask you, can you see the air? Can you hear the silence? Of course you can't, but you know it's there. God is also here, and you will be judged.

You and I want the same things. To feed, clothe and shelter those we love. But, if I allow your family these basic necessities at the expense of my family, then essentially, I become your slave. This, I reject totally. At this moment, I am rebelling with this pen in my hand, but I won't hesitate to put a weapon in it if you refuse peaceful dialogue.

You're probably saying, "He's just some crackpot or radical, some sort of militant. And, he's only one." My brother and sister, and you are whether you believe me or not, black or white, you're my brother and sister. I speak for tens of millions in this nation of America. Think about this, if the citizens you police were happy with your services, would it be a constant need to hire more law enforcement officials? And, give you bigger and better weapons? You're not fighting a foreign enemy. You're at war with your fellow citizens. The one your creed says you are suppose to serve and protect.

How many urban police forces have what they call "zero tolerance" in their cities? Mr. And Ms. Law Enforcement Official, if you have "zero tolerance" for the people that you're suppose to serve and protect, then you're at war with them; because a person has only "zero tolerance" for their enemies.

The people of America, Black and White, aren't happy with you. You are intimidating with your sirens and side arms. A big part of America's population doesn't know who to fear more, the criminal or you. You terrorize the inner cities. I know all isn't well in the ghettos, but the guns we fear are of two types, the misguided brothers and you, the well-directed police.

You see, Mr. and Ms. Police Officer, we brothers on the corners with the out of this world look on our faces, are humans. We don't like the everyday struggle anymore than you, but you hurt us as if we are beasts. Maybe this is how some of you law enforcement officials keep your heads, by believing we're animals of prey.

You say, "Stay off the corners." We say, "Stay out of the hood." Now, the laws are with you, and against us. When we kill with guns, we're called violent criminals. When you kill a human with a gun, you're called a hero. Aren't we both humans killing humans in an endless cycle of violence? You say, men like me are the bad guys, but we're still humans. Your labels may ease your conscience, but will not save your soul.

I'm not asking you for sympathy. I'm explaining why your future is grim if you continually refuse to admit that we're human. Just like you have zero tolerance for our presence on this earth, it'll become a question of survival for us to no longer tolerate your presence.

If you continue to believe big guns and more prisons are the answer, you're making peace impossible. You can't honestly believe you can continue incarcerating human soul after human soul, and nothing will happen. This belief goes against history, and against human nature.

Look at me! You helped in my creation. I came from that place you try to keep from your children's eyes, and hide from their minds. I'm reality. Not a motion picture or a rap song. I'll shoot you if you try and put me in chains, or steal my freedom. Freedom means this much to me. I don't want to harm you, but I refuse to allow you to harm me. I'm a free man, not an enslaved one.

I'm going to spread this gospel of freedom to whoever will listen. Whenever and wherever I can. I'm not going to tell the children you're their enemy, but I will define their enemy. If you fit the description, don't blame the truth. Change the lie.

FRIEND OR ENEMY?

How do you distinguish a friend from an enemy? An elder brother once told me that there are three keys to finding out: (1) go to jail; (2) get sick; or (3) become broke. Now, by me being an outlaw, this question takes on a meaning that is the equivalent to life and earth, and in the past caused me many sleepless nights. Between the threat of white men and all his evil apparatus for death, and wondering who is your friend, you can get lost.

It was a warm, spring day, and I was driving in a green Jeep Cherokee. I was a couple of blocks from the house I shared with my business partners. The police had stopped traffic at the intersection to let the school children cross. I didn't want to wait, so I turned the car out of traffic in order to go another way. Cars were coming so I turned the car back into the line of cars waiting.

When traffic started to move, I drove on. When I got to the intersection, the policeman pulled me over. He was a young Black man like myself. He asked for my license. I told him I didn't have one. He asked me to get out of the car. I got out. He told me to lean my back against the front of the car. He checked the car, and I waited. He said he found nothing "illegal" in the car, but he was going to give me a ticket. I said nothing. He then said he was going to arrest me. I said, "What?" Then told him, "I'll leave the car, walk up the street, and have a friend with a license come move the car." He said he was going to arrest me. I told him, "Not today." He then moved toward me, and I moved toward him. He tried to grab my hands, and I grabbed his hands. He tried to kick me, and I kicked him. We struggled, but he was unable to move me. As we were wrestling, I kept his hands away from his weapon. He kept struggling to take me down, and I kept resisting while talking in his ear. I was asking him, "Why are you doing this, brotha? Why are you doing this to your brotha?"

Then something happened that I didn't expect. Young Black men in sports utility vehicles like mine, Acuras, and a few other high-end cars came driving up. I told them to stay back, that it's okay. I thought they were coming to help me, but I was wrong. They were all police in plain clothes driving nice cars. I never thought cops traveled like this.

All these cops were trying to take me. They were all over me like a pack of wolves. I could see patrol cars pulling up, sirens blaring, and lights swirling. I could see everything. I could even smell them. I had strength I never knew I had, and became faster. My mind was alert in a way that I never thought could be. I felt like a bright light and all the insects were coming to me in a furious way. Then, I lost it. My strength gave out. My mind became dull. I went down, and the cops were cuffing me. We all realized that we witnessed, and were a part of something special. I say special, they said insane.

They asked if I was high. I said, "No." The sergeant, a Black man, looked me in my eye and asked, "Why did you fight? It was just a traffic stop?" I asked him, "Why did the policeman want to arrest me?" I answered for him, "The guy thought it was his right and privilege to arrest me.
I proved it wasn't." I went to jail. The bail was $50, I think.

Some friends came and bailed me out. They were amazed at what happened. They told me the whole police station was buzzing about what happened. But me, I was in deep contemplation.

The whole episode was like a dream to me.
I found myself trying to figure out what happened. I knew intellectually that I decided to resist and rebel, but doing it brought other things to life.

The policemen and policewomen I fought were human. When we were fighting, I could see in their eyes that they were somewhat lost. Not all of them, just some of them. The ones who had a determined look in their eyes were the weakest. The police with the searching looking were the strongest. They didn't want to fight me, but were compelled by forces greater than themselves.

Throughout the whole fight, I was talking. The same way I'd seen Muhammad Ali talk to his opponents in their ear while fighting. Why I did this? I didn't know. I think it was because I had their attention and wanted to talk with them more than fight them.

When I stepped into the street that spring day, I felt a surge run through me. For the first time in this life my soul was completely awakened. While I was fighting and talking, the children were on the sidewalk with their mothers' watching. I could see their faces and feel their thoughts. For this brief moment I had become a part of something greater than me, something that was inside of me, not outside of me. I meditated a lot after this. The girlfriend I had thought I was on the verge of insanity. She was a college girl whose greatest worry was her upcoming final exams and graduation in May. We clearly were not on the same path, so we didn't speak much during this time and not much after this time. I had changed, and the change was happening regardless of those around me believe. I was traveling towards the light inside of me, not the light outside of me.

At this time, I decided to stop going to the mosque. No temple of stones could help me. As a matter of fact, I started to see all buildings built for the worship of God as hypocritical. I thought the money spent to build temples to God would be better spent on feeding the children of God. I didn't go to the café a lot either.

I stayed in my room thinking, meditating, and traveling through my mind. The feeling of my soul completely awakened made everything else trivial and petty in comparison.

It felt electric to fight with all my soul, that which I believed to be wrong. At the same time, I was worried. I never thought it would come to this. I was a few months away from becoming 30 years of age, and didn't have a clear goal. All I had was a feeling inside that I was growing and becoming more than just a man. My definition of what a man is was changing.

Time went by and I settled back into the daily grind of running a business, hoping I could get rid of this feeling. I no longer wanted the fire inside. It felt as if it was going to burn me. Still, creation stops for nothing. When its time for something to happen, it will happen no matter what the odds. I think this is why astrology and forms of oracles are forever popular. People want to know what time it is. They want to know if it is their time.

So, a few weeks later, life took another turn for me. It was a spring night, and the wind was warm and peaceful. The café was filled with Howard University students who were discussing ways they could show support for the unjustly imprisoned Mumia Abu Jamal. I was listening and became very encouraged by the students' activism on all prisoners behalf.

As the meeting was coming to an end, people were eating and drinking coffee and tea. The contractor who did some work on the café, pulled up outside. He double-parked his car, and we started talking. Suddenly, a police patrol car pulled up behind his double-parked car, and a Black police officer got out. He came over to me and asked, "Whose car is this?" The owner of the car, the contractor, said it was his, but the police officer kept his eyes on me. You see, he and I had exchanged words a week earlier about him writing tickets in front of the café. The area was a legal parking area, but police still wrote tickets, blatantly disregarding their own laws.

The police officer looked at me, and I at him. When the contractor started to move his car, the police officer then started to look at the café. He could see inside because the front was all glass. He saw a table with two chairs and a plant outside the café, and said storing furniture on a sidewalk was in violation of the law. I said nothing. He then ordered me to move the furniture inside. I said I would later because customers were inside. He said if I didn't do it immediately, he was going to write me a ticket. I said, "Write the ticket." He looked at me, and said he wasn't going to write me a ticket, but arrest me instead. Of course I told him, he wasn't.

Now, by this time, one of my friends/business partners was at my side. When the police officer tried to grab me, my friend pushed him off of me. The police officer came back at me, and I hit him. He went back, stumbled, grabbed his walkie-talkie, and started saying, "Officer in distress. Officer in distress." He kept his distance, and all of a sudden, from all angles, patrol cars came speeding up with sirens blaring. He pointed to us, and the cops came at us. Some grabbed my friend, and the rest came at me.

I was fighting. I was back in that space again, the space I was in a few weeks ago when I fought the police. My soul awakened. I could see more and more cops coming in all types of cars. The cops were running in the café attacking the students now.

Everyone was screaming, and all I'm thinking is, "I don't want the people in the café to get hurt." So, then I was fighting, and at the same time, pulling police officers off the people. I was on the move. My spirit was free. I felt as if I could fight all of them, and however many more like them.

Then, as quickly as my soul awakened, it stopped. My strength left, and my senses were dulled. Cops were all over my body, but I was still on my feet. While they were holding my arms and legs, a white female cop squared up to me, and hit me in the face. I went crazy at that moment, and then a white male cop hit me on my forehead with his nightstick. All the cops who were holding me, were Black. Blood was all over my eyes, and having blood in my eyes is a feeling I'll never forget. I couldn't see, and my strength was gone.

I went down. They carried me to a patrol car, then to the precinct around the corner.

I was placed in the precinct's holding cell. All the cells were filled with students who the cops arrested. Some were let go from the precinct, while a few of us were kept. All through the night, police officers came to my cell asking, "Why did you fight?" Some asked, "Don't you know you're not supposed to fight the police?" I answered, "Didn't someone tell you, you're not supposed to attack the citizens?"

One cop came by. He was a Sergeant. He told me he was a graduate of Howard University. He asked me what happened, and I told him. He said, "You were wrong." I told him, "I am right."

I showed him what the white cops did to my head, and said he was a fool to enforce laws of white men and women. He told me again that I was wrong. He said he was protecting the community from criminals. I asked, "Then why don't you go and arrest your white boss?" He asked if I thought Black people are completely innocent and can do no wrong? I asked him if he was a Black man and he answered, "Yes." I responded, "Well, you're not innocent, and you're doing something wrong." He shot me a disgusted look and left.

Next, a Black cop wearing a white shirt, a Lieutenant, came in. He looked at me, and said that the President of Howard University called the precinct. I said nothing. He then told me how he hates "little dumb niggas" like me, and if he could, he would kill us all. I said nothing. At that moment, I felt compassion for my older brother. To have such hate for another human, and to have hate for the children of your race is even worse. I told him to leave me. I didn't want to talk to any more police.

The next day we all went to court. While we were waiting, a lot of students from Howard University, and concerned people in the community, packed the courtroom for us. We were released.

I said, "Thank you," then went to my girlfriend's house. She was somewhat concerned, but was very worried about missing a class because she had to wait for me in the courtroom. I knew she cared, but what I was going through, she wasn't a part of. She was a nice young lady, but in that moment I knew we saw life differently.

Life went on. I went back to the café the next day, and the phone was ringing off the hook. I had hundreds of emails from people around the world. The Washington Times newspaper wrote an article about the incident, and people from everywhere were upset. I didn't know so many people and organizations around the world were feeling upset at the injustices that were going on in the world, and I even received an email from a Militia group. I heard about them on the news, and they were portrayed as angry white men and women. I was shocked to read their email. They were very concerned and proud Americans. They believed in freedom, and were questioning America's government the way I was. They were doing it in a different way, but they were questioning.

Lots of lawyers called wanting to represent, but I didn't want to have a martyr trial. I called none of them back. A week or two went by, and the excitement decreased. However, I was still feeling restless. I could feel something coming. Two fights with the police. I had no weapon, and still I lived. I was wondering what was going on. Shit just didn't stop coming. The cops kept harassing and driving by shooting mean looks. They even set up a full roadblock in front of the café one Thursday evening. Said they were checking cars for warrants.

One day I needed to get away from the café, and decided to take a drive. I didn't have a license, but I felt I had to drive. I left the café around 8:00pm, and before I knew it, I was around American University, which is far away from the café. I felt extremely tense, and immediately turned around and headed back to my neighborhood. I drove a block or two when I spot lights of a patrol car on behind me. I stopped the car, but kept the engine running. I rolled up all four windows. A white police officer came up to my window and asked for my driver's license. I told him that I haven't got one. He asked for any identification. I gave him a D.C. Identification Card. He walked to his car, and a few minutes later he returned and ordered me to get out of the jeep. I said, "Officer, if I get out of this car, one of us is going to die because I am not going to jail." He ordered me to get out again, then said, " I know who you are, and I have already called for back up." I rolled up the window.

Again, he ordered me to get out. Then, a couple of patrol cars come toward us with lights spinning and sirens screaming. I knew I either had to fight or die, so I decided to fight, but I quickly had to decide how to fight. I didn't want to fight there, in a white neighborhood with all white cops. I decided to make it back to my territory, then fight.

I put in the Tupac tape I had just made earlier. "My Ambitions as a Rider" was the first song. I put the Cherokee in drive, and mashed on the accelerator. It was on! I didn't know how many cop cars were in pursuit of me, but I was a long ways from home.

Suddenly, my soul awakened again. I saw my final destination. I saw the route to take. I drove through Georgetown (a section of D.C), and then I was on Wisconsin honking my horn. The streets were packed with cars, and the cops were still behind me. I made a left at the corner of Wisconsin and M Street. I was speeding down M Street, and must've had seven or ten cars following me. Somehow I found myself a block away from the White House. I turned left, and cops were coming from everywhere. I didn't hear the sirens, and the lights didn't bother me. I was very alert. I was driving extremely fast, but being very cautious. I didn't want to hurt anyone, or hit another car. The cops were talking to me through speakers on their cars, but I wasn't fazed by it.

Tupac was rapping, "Only God Can Judge Me," and I thought, "He is right. Fuck these people. No so-called authority will ever rule over me. I want to be free." I was wondering, "Will I die tonight?" I couldn't feel death because too much life was running through my veins. I was thinking, "Mama is going to be real mad about this." I was at peace as I kept driving, doing doughnuts in the street as I drove through downtown D.C. I was floating on a cloud.

I knew God was with me, flowing through me. I reached the café. That was where I wanted to make my stand, but I saw lots of young Black people in the street. The café was packed, and I remembered that across the street Erykah Badu was performing at the 9:30 Club.

She had just finished the first show, and the second show was going to start soon.

I decided not to risk all those people's lives. It was my fight, not theirs. I knew the cops wanted to shoot me, and would shoot whoever was in between. I yelled at a friend, "I'm going to the Masjid," then did a 360° doughnut to shake the cops and sped up the street toward the Howard University Hospital.

I knew the area well. I cut through the parking lot and came out on the other side. The cops were still coming. I lost one, and another came from nowhere. I passed by one of Howard's dorms named Slowe Hall. I saw people I knew, and they knew the car. When they all saw the cops, their faces filled with amazement. It was like a movie that came to life. I kept driving until I was a block from the Masjid Muhammad. I used to attend Jumah there every Friday.

I pulled the car up as close as I could to the Masjid, and jumped out. The police were chasing me on foot, but I got them. I was very fast that night. I felt as if I could fly. I ran through the Masjid doors and yelled, "Allahu Akbar." Some brothers were praying, and were upset that I interrupted their prayer. They all knew me, and asked what was wrong? I told them. They went outside and saw lots of cops with guns drawn. They told me to go in a room off to the side. Cops came rushing inside the Masjid with guns looking for me. The brothers were yelling, "This is a place of Allah." The cops relented and went outside.

The brothers asked me what happened, again. I told them, and they all knew about my troubles with the police. They decided to help me. They got the Imam (leader of the Masjid). He knew me well, and often came by the café for a cup of coffee with other brothers. I told him what happened. He asked why I came to the Masjid? I told him, "Allah led me here." He looked in my eyes and told me to go downstairs. He went outside to talk with the police. They told him that they wanted me. He let one of the cops come in to speak with me. The cop told me to come outside. I said, "No!" He looked at the Imam, and the Imam asked him to step outside. Then, the Imam looked at me and said that I had to leave the Masjid. I looked at him and said, "Okay."

I then proceeded to prepare to go outside. He asked what was I going to do? I said, "Fight them." He looked in my eyes. I looked in his. He said nothing. I continued. I laced up my boots, tucked my shirt in, and tightened my belt. I started to go outside, and right before I touched the door, the Imam asked me to stop. I stopped. He told me to wait, and then went back outside. Another cop came in with him. This cop was Muslim. He told me they were not going to arrest me, and that they just needed my name and social security number.

I told him my name and birth date. I asked him why weren't they trying to arrest me? He said some legal stuff that to this day I don't understand. I just knew the police were gone and I was alive after all that had happened.

I stepped outside and my senses returned to their usual state. My soul was no longer awake. I just broke down in tears. The tears just came out.

I hadn't been afraid. Just felt different. I was ashamed to be crying in front of all those men. It was unbecoming, but still the tears flowed.

Eventually, I stopped crying. I thanked the Imam, and all the brothers. Someone drove me home. I couldn't sleep. I sat up expecting the police to come rushing in at any moment, but no police came. I just lay awake in my bed wondering, "How did it come to this?"

WHY WON'T THEY BELIEVE ME

Why won't they believe me when I tell them
I'm suffering the truth?
Why do they listen to words of the ones who
hate them, but ignore my love?
Why do they work for him who enslaved them?
Why do they kill for him who kills them?
Why do they consume his images of sin?
Why do they trust him to educate the babies
when he kills the babies?
Why do they submit to his laws, when the laws
oppress them?
Why won't they believe me?

I FALL APART

On May 16, 1997, I turned 30 years of age and I was happy to be alive, but my future seemed blurry. I knew I still had some traveling to do, but where and when, I didn't know. I never would've guessed I was going back to jail again.

I had been out of jail for over three years. I had done a few things, but had lots more to do. All of my battles with police had taken my attention away from the café. The business was in bad shape. Bills had piled up. I hadn't managed the money well. Rather, I let other people manage my money. Things were going down.

The café was my base of operation, and so many people shared it with me. So many children used the café as a refuge from the cruel world. I didn't want the café to close, but I was behind on the rent and my business partners had lost interest after all that had happened. Still, I wanted the café to stay open. So, I decided to return to my old ways. I lost faith in me again. I no longer trusted God. Although I had experienced a few brief moments of enlightenment, I didn't believe.

Everyone around me seemed to be going deeper into this world. Friends thought I was crazy. My girlfriend had graduated and moved back to New York City. I was in debt, and had court dates coming up. I wanted out of this circle in the worst way, and decided to write a business check knowing that the money wasn't in the account. I consciously and willingly had broken one of the money game laws. I didn't care. I had good reasons, I believed. All I could say when I was arrested was, "Fuck this world." I no longer cared about this country, or this world. Corruption and greed was everywhere. The more I screamed for peace, the more people laughed at me or ran away from me.

When I found myself in D.C. jail, I realized I had come to the end of this road. All my friends and business partners left me hangin'. One business partner even told me on the phone while I was in D.C. jail, "Fuck you, punk." Needless to say, I was pissed and hurt. I also wondered if I had brought all this on myself. All I've been told from the cradle was,

"You only fight injustice when the unjust allow you to." I was supposed to use tactics that had been approved by the government. Any form of protest outside of the accepted ones was deemed to be wrong and backwards.

I found myself once again in jail waiting to see a federal judge because I once again broke federal laws. I was upset, but I could only try and hold myself together. What money I had was gone. My so-called friends/business partners had stolen everything I had. These brothers even took the new plumbing and furnace out of the café to sell.

I told my court appointed attorney that I did not want to go to trial. I would plead guilty. The prosecutor was surprised that I pleaded guilty. The judge put me in a half way house in D.C. while I waited to be sentenced. I went to check out my house, and found that everything was gone. My now, ex-girlfriend helped me out some. We were still friends, but on different paths. She had her life to live. She had a college degree now, and new doors were opened up to her. I was glad for her because that was what she wanted. I was stuck in what felt like Hell. No money, no friends, and nothing but court dates to look forward to. Plus, I knew I was going back to jail. Life looked bleak, but, even though I was down, I wasn't out.

I decided to spend my time in the Library of Congress. I hadn't been in a library in a long time. I went into the Great Reading Room. Sad and alone, I decided to get a book. The Library of Congress is a unique library. It has a copy of every book printed in the United States, and every book imported into the United States. I read everyday. I read newspapers and magazines. I watched movies and listened to music in the Music Room. One song stands out from that time, "What a Wonderful World" by Louis Armstrong. He made me feel good. The song pointed out the joy of the simple things in life. I started to read books about business, and found that a lot of business people found it unrewarding, but used their businesses to help the world as best they could.

The most rewarding of my studies at the Library of Congress was History. Not just American History, but the world's history. My soul was weary, and my heart was weak. I wanted to know how the world got in this condition. I read about Asian history.

I became aware of their great philosophers, Kings and Queens. I read Asian novels that had been translated into English. Asian culture was fascinating, yet their culture seemed to point to a deeper origin.

I read about American people before it was called America. Members of my family are Native American. I was glad to learn about this part of us.

I read about the Latin people in their many shades of color. Yet, all I read pointed to a deeper origin. That origin was Africa.

The Library of Congress had books about Africa that I never knew existed. I got a chance to study Greek philosophy at its origin. All the Greeks were taught in Africa, Egypt in particular. In studying Egypt, I found the greatest repository of the world's history. The more I learned of Egypt, the greater my understanding of my life became. I knew, vaguely, that many men and women had traveled the righteous path, but I never thought that an entire civilization was built by a soul-searching people.

Learning that many millennium before Jesus Black men and women had discovered the secret of immortality. It wasn't a pill or a fountain of water. Nor was it a magical spell. The secret is that life itself is eternal. Every step we take is our choice. We either chose righteousness, or we accept injustice.

God is inside all of us, and everything we see. The Pharaohs of Egypt were called the Sons of God. It didn't mean that we are not children of God. But, that the Pharaohs consciously evolved into the consciousness of God. There is a saying that explains this: A person who is traveling asks the question, "What is a Man?" The Pharaoh answers, "A Mortal God." Then the traveler asks, "What is God?" The Pharaoh answers, ""An Immortal Man."

In other words, the truth is eternal. And, a man who chooses to live the truth no matter what anyone says, no matter what the threat of punishment, is immortal and his deeds are eternal. This is why Jesus is immortal and truly the Son of God. He knew the truth. He learned it from the home of God, Egypt. He lived the truth no matter what any government priest, merchant, or temple said. He lived the truth. This I understood, yet I still was stuck in Hell. The federal courts don't care about truth. The courts care about upholding the laws of mortal men, in particular white men. The truth of this made me sick.

My body started to swell with bumps. They started on the right side of my neck. Then, I started getting pounding headaches at night, and started to lose weight. Yet, I had to stay alive. I didn't have much money. The only money I had was the few bucks my grandmother sent me. I ate McDonalds double cheeseburgers almost everyday. At night, in the halfway house, I felt like dying. I read the Psalms in the morning. David's sorrow I felt was mine.

I prayed for strength. Still, my body was falling apart. In November of 1997, Judge Royce C. Lamberth sentenced me to 19 months in a federal corrections facility. I had a year and a half of jail time before me. I was alone, dying on the inside and barley enough money to eat everyday.

On January 6, 1998, I arrived at Fort Dix, New Jersey to do my time at Fort Dix Federal Correctional Institute. Fort Dix FCI was an old Army base. It had a fence around it with barbed wire. This wasn't a camp.

By the time I arrived at Fort Dix, my body was swollen with bumps. The doctor who examined me took some test and told me two days later I had cancer - Hodgkin's disease to be exact. My lymph nodes were swollen all over my body. The doctor took more tests. A cancer specialist looked at me. He told me I needed treatment immediately or I would die in six months. I had memorized the "Temptation of Christ" when I was a boy. Now, I knew why.

This was the test of my life. I knew that I was being tempted. I had to choose my path. Put my life on the line. Medical science in this western world has been developed out of the mind of humans who believe some humans are born slaves. This medical science knows nothing of the human soul. It is preoccupied with the human body. Like a slave master, this medicine doesn't care about the soul. It wants the body. The soul is a nuisance, and therefore, there is no discussion of the soul in western medicine.

Thoughts don't have power in western medicine. Daily pills that have been tested on laboratory rats have power. Institutionalized injustice can never be the cause of illness and disease to a slave master. Only the laziness and ungratefulness of the slave is the cause. Therefore, give the slave a pill, and have a magician with a degree prescribe the pill or cut the body open and the slave will get better.

At Fort Dix, I met a good brother named, Arnold Griffith. Big Griff, is what we called him. Griff had been convicted of drug dealing when he was 23. He was sentenced to 10 years in prison. Had the drugs been powder cocaine instead of crack, he would have gotten probation. But, crack laws reflect the racism in America. White men sell powder, Black men sell crack, which is powder cocaine rocked up. The media told America it was the ghetto boyz in the "hood" who were destroying America. Although it eventually came out that white men in the U.S. military and U.S. corporations are the real drug dealers.

Anyway, Griff was a student of good health and positive thoughts. He gave me some books about the diets of we humans. One book was, "A Diet for a New America." This book showed me that Elijah Muhammad's "How to Eat to Live" was prophetic. Elijah was telling we Black folks that our diet was the diet of a slave, and that most of our illnesses could be put in check if we changed our diet and gained knowledge of self. Griff is a free man now, and a friend for life. The doctors kept telling me I was dying. But, I was feeling like I was starting to come back to life. I asked myself "Who is God?" I answered with an eternal, "Me." Believing in our heart, in the spirit, the force that guided our growth from a blood clot to a fully live spirit in flesh is the true healer.

Men and women of any color can never heal you completely. We can offer guidance and comfort to each other, but the healing begins and ends with you, the human.

"Where there is a way between a traveler and his destination, he can hope to reach it, but if there is no way, or if he does not know which way to take, what is the good of knowing the destination? Now, there is one way, and one way alone that can save us from all aberrations, the way which is both God and man – God as the goal and man as the means to reach it."

St. Augustine, The African Saint,
***City of God* Book XI**

STRATEGY OF AN OUTLAW

To me, the goal of my life is to reach God's house. It's a lofty goal, the loftiest, but what else should a human strive for. As an Outlaw, your strategy must be tight, and never should your strategy negate the Creator. Police, Marshalls, FBI Agents, CIA and whoever else are strong, but believe me brothers and sisters, God is far more powerful.

Now, before I get into my strategy for victory over Babylon, I feel it's best to explain Babylon's strategy. Their strategy is plain and simple, "intimidation."

This strategy is a good one, but bound for defeat because history proves that any nation, which believes intimidation of its citizens, is the best way to keep a nation, will fall eventually. When you intimidate or bully someone, it builds an incredible amount of animosity in the victims of this cruel virtue. This animosity will eventually turn to frustration then anger, and eventually rebellion.

The best examples of intimidation of Africans in America that I can think of was in our period of chattel slavery. Slavery was straight intimidation. But, from time to time some brothers and sisters got to the stage of rebellion. Nat Turner, a slave preacher who had a vision from God that it was time to rebel and didn't hesitate to acknowledge the prophecy and rebelled. Although it didn't fully succeed, it sparked the imagination of a people.

Harriet Tubman and her magnificent underground railroad is another example. Harriet Tubman was and is the outlaw's model for success. She broke the law to free herself, then broke it several more times coming back and forth to free her people. Also, Frederick Douglas is a shining star in our history of rebellion. I quote him when he speaks of his strategy for victory, he said, "On the plantation, the slave who got whipped the easiest, got whipped the most." Is there anything more straight to the point? This holds true today in America. This nation fucks with those who have the least and are the least able to protect and defend themselves.

Now, any nation that trusts intimidation as a means of control, rather than justice, is headed for destruction. I know America has courts of law that supposedly dispense justice, but the intimidation factor is in full effect in America's courts. Those special and privileged individuals who can afford a proper legal defense will get justice. But, most Americans who deal with the justice system aren't one of the few privileged. They're part of the many poor, therefore, they get no justice in America. The potential for injustice is greater when you're Black. What a world we live in.

I believe the outlaws I mentioned above got to the point of rebellion because they were clearly in opposition of white authorities. I'm sure there were lots of Black people against these outlaws. The usual reasons for not joining the outlaws were given: "It's not so bad here on the plantation. There's a better way to do this." Yet, this better way never presents itself. Or, how about, "The man will get you. See how he got so and so when he tried?" This is another part of the intimidation. The idea that someone already tried, and I got them, so you better not try nigga!

Let me tell you, people, white people and America don't rule the world. And, the world is getting tired of their tricks. Oh yeah, please allow me to give an example of the intimidation factor overcome in recent history:

On July 1, 1997, Hong Kong, which had been colonialized by Great Britain for over 150 years, returned to China, it's motherland. Now, you know Britain didn't leave because it was wrong to occupy land that wasn't theirs. They left because the Chinese were no longer intimidated by the British. They sacrificed many decades to get to this point, and overcame just as many obstacles, but their foreign ruler left because it became impossible to rule. The people of China aren't scared of White people. Take notes Black people, there are people on the planet who fight the White people when they act unjustly. Don't let the media fool you with all of its pomp and circumstance. England left because they had no other choice. Not because they became enlightened on the subject of Human Rights and a nations sovereignty. This never stopped them before, China became an outlaw nation in the first part of the 20th Century, and became totally free by the end of the century.

Some may say that they don't enjoy the freedom of democracy because they are communist. This is arrogance on the speaker's part. It assumes that the Chinese people can't rationalize slavery from freedom or that one political system is right for every nation. I've read many newspaper articles and heard countless tales of China's opposition to human rights, but I laugh when I hear news reporters crying out about China's brutality. Why? Because all I have to do is walk outside my door and I can see armed men in blue with guns patrolling my neighborhood, who've been trained to kill the citizen who disagrees with them. Remember, most instances of brutality are against citizens who work and pay taxes, not drug dealers.

I wonder, is it a human rights violation when over one third of a race's men are in jail, waiting to go, or on probation? If a country's laws are causing so many of its citizens to lose their freedom, and the law was supposedly written to increase freedom, is this a just law? It sounds more like a conspiracy, not a law.

To me, America doesn't have the authority to call me a criminal or the bad guy. I refuse to accept their labels as my name. Feel me, young soldiers?

Your freedom is precious. Don't give it up for anything or any amount of time.

As I stated at the beginning of this, I would discuss the outlaw's strategy, although I somewhat digressed, I'll return now to the main subject, which is strategy.

Now, my strategy has three parts: Education, Advance and Defend. The first part, education, is the foundation of an outlaw's strategy. A proper education is one that brings out a person's natural genius and innate sense of justice.

As a child, the education I received prepared me to accept the values of America, even when these values were clearly self-destructive and against my very existence as a human being. Well into high school and through my college years, I rebelled against this fake education. I believe it's all that saved me from the living hell of ignorance. I was blessed that I ran to books instead of the streets. Well, I liked the streets too, but books explained what I was seeing and doing, and raised my expectation of what I could do.

My time in prison was my real time for education. I had lots of time, and I had read Malcolm X's autobiography, and used his prison experience as a model for my own stay in prison. I came in contact with books that I had heard of vaguely, but never thought to explore. Before this period, I couldn't see how books written hundreds of years ago could help my situation. I discovered that in ancient times, humans struggled desperately for the best way to co-exist. Most of America's constitutional rhetoric comes from such books, as *"Leviathan"* by Thomas Hobbes, *"On Liberalism"* by Alan Locke, *"Republic"* by Plato, and many more. I also discovered that all of this ancient European knowledge was actually, ancient African knowledge and wisdom, and had been misunderstood by the Greeks.

I also found the new books being written on African history highly enlightening. Such as, Cheikh Anta Diop's *"African Origin of Civilization, Myth or Reality."* This brother, Diop, was a genius by all standards of the word, and he was an outlaw in my eyes because he rebelled against the lie that we Africans had no history. His conviction and belief in his African blood's greatness caused him to stand up against the prevailing educational power structure. He mastered many disciplines, all with the thought of using his knowledge to prove to Africans worldwide that the word African means something beyond slavery and violence.

Carter G. Woodsons' *"Mis-Education of the Negro,"* not quite new being it was written in the 1930's, proved my belief that the education I had received in America had not done what it said it would do (free me from ignorance), but as he said, "taught the Black person to make a back door even when there wasn't one." He believed that we have to build industries to feed, cloth and shelter ourselves, and that high salary jobs in corporate America would increase the standard of living for a few, but would do nothing for the many. I agree with him whole-heartedly.

When a race has mastered the art of transformation, they are able to plant a seed in mother earth, nurture that seed to harvest. Then take the harvested thing and manufacture it into an item for human use. Then distribute this finished product in an orderly fashion to the market. Then retail the product at a reasonable price for all who need the product can purchase the product.

Now, let me use a real product that we Africans in America know all too well, king cotton. Cotton is planted then harvested. Then the cotton is manufactured into a shirt. The shirt is then shipped (distribution) to the stores to be sold (retail), and then the consumer/citizen purchases the finished product for their use.

We Africans in America overwhelmingly are only involved in the retail end. In other words, we just buy the shirt and haven't any idea how the shirt came to us.

Now, what I've just explained is the art of transformation. When the art of transformation is mastered, a people can build a nation. This is true independence. Hustling drugs or whatever else we can hustle, leaves us only on the retail end of transformation. We'll always be victims if this continues.

To all my young brothers and sisters, you can learn the art of transformation without going to college. You can learn this by doing it. You have to explore the art of transformation in detail. Just as Carter G. Woodson stated in "Mis-Education of the Negro" the Black person is being mis-educated in the universities. Now, don't get arrogant and say, fuck college and school, but become humble. Respect this art of transformation and it will respect you. If you are in college, learn it. If you're not in college, learn it. Once we've mastered it. We'll transform this cruel world we were raised in.

Allow me to give an example of how this transformation game lays. Let's say a sister wants to sell T-shirts with the word "Freedom" on the front, and "Justice" on the back.

Now, she should not start by purchasing some T-shirts form a T-shirt wholesaler. She should first find out how T-shirts are made. She should look outside of America for this information, also. Find out how much cotton is used in the production of one shirt (1, 100, 1,000 or 10,000 pounds). She should know what kind of machinery is used in making the T-shirts. She should also know how much the machines that make the shirt cost and who makes the machines that makes the shirts. She should know how much shipping cost over the road by trucks, over the rails by trains, over the sea by boat, and in the air by plane.

The sister should do research of T-shirt manufacturers in other countries, such as various nations in Africa, China, Indonesia, Philippines and Mexico. She can write a letter or call the embassies of these nations and request the information. She'll be surprised what she discovers. Remember, the nations I named are trying to master the art of transformation too, and will understand and respect your spirit. You are all of color after all.

If the sister needs money, she can try banks, but you know how they treat us. I suggest getting some of her fellow sister friends together. Now, what I'm about to say may sound wild, but think about it with an open mind.

I suggest each girl go to the hustlers in the neighborhood all of you know, and get your start up capital from them. Instead of asking for clothes, cars and material things, ask for help in making clothes for your children, their children. You're going to make money and it's a way for each sister involved to clothe her children and others for a minimal price.

I know some are saying, "How can he condone using drug money to build industry for Black people? Drug money is blood money!"

Whoever would say this is right. Drug money is blood money, but does it stop all the car dealers from taking it? Does it stop all the high clothing and shoe manufacturers from taking it? I say, No.

I know they openly court this drug money to fatten their pockets and feed, cloth and shelter their families at the expense of our people's destruction.

I'm saying you can't stop some brothers from hustling. Not the threat of prison or death will deter them. I say, "Don't stop them from hustling, elevate their hustle." If a young brother or sister has the courage to face police, an angry community, and the threat of death, they have something good inside of them. It just needs to be elevated.

That's why I say, "education is the first part and the foundation of an outlaw's strategy." Education teaches a person how to make something from nothing, and how to turn a negative situation into a positive one.

In defense of my recommendation to all who still disagree, I direct your attention to the CIA (Central Intelligence Agency). They've delivered all cocaine that has come into America. They fund all of their covert activities from taxpayer's money and transforming drugs into dollars and dollars into weapons and influence.

The government of America taxes the manufacturers of alcohol and cigarettes, which kill far more Americans than illegal drugs. And, all the revenue from the taxes supposedly goes to better the nation. I say, why don't we use our negative situation and create something positive? I say, stop condemning the young hustlers and respect the spirit of someone who wants more from a land that doesn't want to give he/she anything. They didn't come out dreaming of riches. It was a dream taught to them. Now, we can unlearn this bullshit, and learn the art of transformation. This is the beauty of a true education. It doesn't make you judgmental.

It makes you compassionate. When you know something is wrong, don't blame the wrongdoer. Focus on the wrong done. Solve the problem. Don't create another one.

So, to end this first part of the outlaw strategy of Education, let me stress reading, observation, discussion and action as the road to your goal of freedom. Many will discourage you in your studies if you're not in college, but don't get discouraged by these ignorant people. Be brave and study. This first part is the most difficult to get through, but it's the foundation. Just like a house, it's only as good as it's foundation. Your education will strengthen you in times of despair. It will enable you to solve the problems you're bound to face in life. But, most of all, your education will give you hope in the future. Make you believe in more than what is given to you. You'll see the world is yours to be shared with others. Also, a true education enables the holder to see through the tricks of the enemy. This is possibly the most important use of an education. It teaches you to see in the dark when others are bumping into walls.

As I stated earlier, America and white people don't rule the world. They trick the world. They trick the world by the use of their media (television, radio, films, newspapers, magazines and books), and even more increasingly the Internet. I can't possibly know all the tricks now, or the ones to come, but through the study of history, I know they're very tricky. Knowing a person or group is tricky is half the battle in discovering the trick because if you know they got tricks, you can look for the trick in their presentation. I could write volumes about the tricks of America that have made our history as Africans in America full of tragedy after tragedy, but this book is about moving on while acknowledging the past.

My education opened my eyes to all the possibilities of ways to achieve freedom, but everywhere I looked I saw conflict. So, this inevitable conflict leads me to the second part of the outlaw strategy – how to advance, once you realize you must.

To me, advance means any progress made in solving a problem. I like the term positive action. Now, my problem is I want freedom, but live in a nation that sees my freedom as a crime unless my freedom has been sanctioned by the powers that be.

As a human being in his right mind, I feel the deep desire to advance in all areas of my life - spiritually, mentally, physically, and scientifically. I often feel like a child when I contemplate the vastness of God's creation. The precision and the creativity in the universe is mesmerizing. There are so many things to experience in this world we all live in. I find it disgusting that a few humans want to prevent the many from experiencing the greatness of creation. I don't know why injustice always finds fertile breeding ground in the hearts of some men and women. I suppose that's a question I'll never get the answer to because history shows unjust thoughts and actions are a part of human history. But, I believe Allah uses these unjust thoughts and actions of the few to call the many into action and service of all that is good in creation.

I quote from a man named, Victor Hugo, who sums up this feeling of mine. He said, "All it takes for evil to triumph is for good to do nothing." This call for good people to do something is the spirit and core of an outlaw's theory of advancement. To me, America's history is littered with crime after crime against humanity. Not just against we Africans in America, but against all the many races in this land. From the Native American destruction and African chattel slavery to the systematic mis-education of the white race throughout America. This last point may prove to be in the future, America's greatest crime. Now, there have always been good people in America, but in my generation they seem to be more silent than ever. Even though the continuing moral decay of the nation demands they stand up and be noticed.

Now, evil can never advance. It simply destroys. To advance means to build. If you the reader take notice when ever evil is rampant in America, good ideas are discredited, good intentions are looked down upon and honest effort in solving the nations problems is interpreted as being soft.

The 90's prove this point. This is the era where prisons are looked upon as a means of advancement. This can be proved by the rapid construction of prisons.

How any society moves to the conclusion that incarcerating massive numbers of its citizenry is advancing on the problem of crime is amazing. The last nation to use this tactic was South Africa pre a free Mandela. At the height of Apartheid, 300,000 young Black men and women were incarcerated. There were 33 million Africans and 3 million whites in South Africa. This was in 1987.

Here in America, in 1997, there are over 1,000,000 Black men and women incarcerated and millions more on probation, waiting to go, on trial, on bond. Believe me reader, this is not advancing, this shows a nation that has given up on implementing its most basic ideas.

To advance in these chaotic and confusing times, it takes courage and creativity. You may think that by speaking out against the spreading evil, you will be outcast, but you will be surprised at who agrees and supports you. I'm not saying a person has to ally 10,000 in front of her or him to be effective. I believe justice advances one person at a time.

As an outlaw, I advance by thinking, then putting my thoughts into action. This last part is crucial, the action part. Sometimes I feel very comfortable thinking, and I believe in what I think, but it's hard to start the action at times. Then, I always remember that cowards never start, and weaklings fall along the way.

So, I simply start. This may sound haphazard, but it's the only way to advance for me. I never know what anything really is until I engage it. I utilize this theory in all my human relations, scientific endeavors, and spiritual searching. I don't fear any human, so why should I not openly interact with all humans.

Science makes the unknown, known. Lack of courage in this arena will cause a person to become stagnant while the rest of the world advances. So, I respect the space exploration technology and all the new computer technology, but in a world of confusion I know these technological advances have the potential to do a tremendous amount of god for humanity, or can be the cause of increased suffering, so I engage science to know.

Spiritually, I advance by constant prayer. Although I don't belong to any one religion, I respect any religion that acknowledges that all creation started from omnipotent, omnipresent, omni-powerful being beyond human comprehension. Whatever name you may call the Creator of the universe, I'm with you if you acknowledge these fundamental truths. Even if you don't, I'll kick it with you, and listen to you.

Spirituality plays a tremendous part in my life, it's my compass in this crossed up world. Any strength of blessing I have came from God. I acknowledge this as often as possible. I'm not afraid of death because I live my life as if every step I take, every breath I take, is a prayer for immortality in heaven.

My life on this earth is finite, but my soul is infinite, and I will be judged by the only being that can judge me, God. So, I advance in this world. Making plans and always accepting the reality that death is imminent. I always try and keep good thoughts in my head, and even though I get tested daily I try my best to maintain. I'm not perfect. I make mistakes, but as an outlaw, mistakes can mean death or prison. But, as stated earlier, I believe every negative situation can be used for the positive. So, even my mistakes can be turned around. So, I carry on daily.

The last part is Defense. The best defense is an almighty offense. Never run away from your enemy, run at your enemy. Even if you must retreat, make sure the retreat is a circle not a line. You must return to do battle again. Don't stop trying, the universe blesses he or she that try to do what is holy. And what is most holy is the truth. If the truth is, you must fight to save your family, take action, defend your truth, but be sure to let all other truths live.

An outlaw uses education, advancement, and defense, to get free and stay free. Rest in peace, fight in peace, live in peace.

Our Misery

There are over a million of we young Black
males in the cells in our land of birth.
I wonder how many millions profit from our
misery.
We young Black men and women are the real
economic jumpstart.
Our misery creates jobs for the low educated,
low income, high school and college graduate.
Our misery is the energy behind countless
songs and movies.
Our misery is legendary.
It sells worldwide.
Our misery gets a politician elected and re
elected.
But, the day is coming when we'll stop being
in misery.
I wonder if all the ones who profit from our
misery will rejoice in our happiness.

LAWS OF NATURE/HUMAN NATURE

A policeman shot himself Friday night. Yesterday, while I was out and about in the community, it was all people were talking about, or should I say, laughing about. I heard not one person say anything remotely close to a regret. People said lots of things but not, "I'm sorry for him and his family." This reaction to a death of someone who supposedly is here to protect the people speaks clearly to the state of relations between police and the people they supposedly protect.

I could speculate on why these feelings exist, but what good would that do? Crime will always be here because human laws seek to control human nature, which is the Law of Nature, and it can't be over-ridden by any human or creation of humans. I don't like murder, rape, molestation, and a host of other human crimes, but every human is different because of their nature. Some people are born homosexual. Is it a far stretch to believe that someone can be a natural born killer? I think not.

I know the laws of humans, at their best, try to create a safe society for as many as possible. But the laws simply point out what is wrong in human society. It can't stop the law of nature. Deterrence is a key word in today's society, but how do you, we, deter a law of nature? A person's nature is their gift from God. It is part of their being, their genetic makeup.

Using the Bible as proof, I point to Cain and Able whose mother and father were the first humans. Cain killed - murdered his brother, Able. Cain acted in harmony with his nature. Yet, his mother and father never committed murder. Cain's nature was that of a murderer, and he murdered.

If laws would've existed, then Cain still would've murdered his brother, except he would've done it with more finesse, or found someone with the identical nature as he and paid that person to do it. The law would've been broken, and the murder still would've been performed. This is just one example, but there are millions of events and happenings that prove that the law of nature will be obeyed at all cost, and no matter what the risk or punishment.

What I'm pointing out is the failure of human law. It seeks to punish a person for acting in accordance with their nature. Therefore, these laws of humans will forever be broken. But, there is hope. The nature of a person cannot be changed, but it can be lifted by upward education. Education without knowledge of self as the goal is not a cure because if a person has a murderous or rapacious nature, education will only refine the nature. So that when an "educated" person murders, it will be more sophisticated. Or, in the worst-case scenario, that person becomes a head of state and propels a nation into war thereby killing millions instead of one. This kind of education is harmful.

I'm talking about upward education - the civilization of the person. The only way to civilize a human is to reveal the human to him or herself. Not by hiding the self, the nature. Or, at its most barbaric, trying to punish the nature. This type of education requires frank and honest discussion about life.

The foundation of all western civilization is based upon repression of the human nature, therefore, it follows that these nations have not become civilized. They may have a civilized veneer, but a closer look reveals barbarism at its worst.

Example: Technology. Technology is the one constant in any human society. In a society that is going upward, the technological advances will be made for improvement of social relations, which is good, because it's well understood that humans are social beings. Therefore, any technology that improves this most basic of human natures is an upward movement. It will strengthen the family, and in turn improve society, which is social.

In a pseudo civilization, all major technological advances will come from the military complex. This technology will never make society better or be the impetus for an upward movement. It will only reinforce the pseudo civilization. A bigger more efficient murdering machine will be created, i.e. bombs, missiles and lasers. Granted, this technology will trickle down to the society, but it will not push it upwards. It will create better ways of existing in the pseudo civilization, but it will not make the pseudo civilization real.

As an outlaw, knowing my nature makes me naturally in conflict with the laws that uphold such a society. As an outlaw, I seek to become civilized. I know that the worst human defects flow through my veins as through all humans. But in a civilized state of being, I try and use these defects for upward movement, and it's been done throughout history. In Sun Tzu's *Art of War*, he said, *"Kill one, to scare a thousand."* This is a civilized person speaking and teaching. A barbarian will kill a thousand knowing that one would have sufficed, and then call the other 999 dead, "collateral damage". This is uncivilized and I will not join such ridiculousness.

Sun Tzu knew that murder was something to avoid, but did not try and repress it. That's why the preceding quote was written. It utilized murder for upward movement. Never saying murder is good, but acknowledging its existence and using it. It's also why Sun Tzu said in the "Art of War" that, *"the best Generals are the ones who win without fighting one battle."* He was an outlaw in his day to many, now he is a sage of wisdom today.

PART TWO

COMRADES

I was born 10,000 years before the human
thought appeared.
My parents tease me about my age.
Rather they make light of it to impress the
stupidity of time and space.
I'm an Angel, a Spirit.
All of creation is Spirit, yet very few parts of
creation know they are Spirit.
Most believe they are what they see.

THE GREAT CHANGE

The great change of the ages is upon us. I hear all the panic and feel the confusion on the streets, yet this great change that will happen is the most beautiful and spiritual times in all of human counting. We must remember that we Africans discovered the movement of the heavens and all the celestial bodies. It took us countless millennium to find our way out of ignorance. It wasn't a one-time effort that discovered this knowledge of time keeping. Unlike the Greeks, we had no one to plagiarize. Through the truthfulness of our effort and sincerity, we embraced the light.

Countless millennium before Christianity, Islam, Judaism, Buddhism, Shintoism, Taoism, Hinduism, and any other religion that any human can claim, we Africans knew the great and eternal Creator. We passed on our knowledge to all who came with humility to seek the truth. All the prophets benefited from our soul searching on their way to true and exact knowledge of the universe.

Many have tried to claim our soul searching as theirs, but the truth can't be hidden for long. This is written. So, here we find ourselves at the changing of an age. Remember that each age consists of 2,160 years, and each great year comes approximately every 26,000 years. Does all this seem great? Well, it should because this knowledge of the heavens took countless great years to discover.

The age that we are leaving is the Age of Pisces, and the age we are entering is the Age of Aquarius. The names that I've just named are the greek translation of the original African names. You see, we Africans are Soul Survivors to the highest degree. The fear and panic that is being propagated is coming from those who know that their time is up. Those souls that have deceived the human family during the pass 2000 years know their time is up. This was written thousands of years before the birth of an African disciple named Jesus who became one of the many Sons of God. He carried the light of the ages to those who dwelled in ignorance. The wisdom is eternal, and the resurrection comes to whoever believes in the wisdom he imparted to the weak and ignorant. The bible reads, "The weak and meek shall inherent the Earth." The other part is, "The strong in heart and soul shall inherent Heaven."

It's wartime to all of you who feel this message. Not the war of deceivers, but war of the righteous. The weak want a war of steel weapons and chemicals concocted out of the mind of a human deluded by their own fantasies of greatness. The strong must follow the way of heaven - the way of the heart. The path is full of obstacles, but help is only a thought away. Don't trip; the Creator is forever in your heart. While Men of God preach the word, the

Word of God is dwelling in your heart waiting to be embraced. There are no mysteries in the universe, just the illusions of the mind.

We are living in the most special of times. The choice must be made brothers and sisters. Watch the signs of the universe and stay in the present moment. The past is behind you. The future is a creation of the present. The ever-living moment is all that is real, and it holds all the potential of creation. Believe in the power that keeps the sun forever burning, the love that keeps the earth forever loving its sons and daughters, and the compassion that the Creator of all gives openly and freely to those who would dare to try.

THE HATE WE CARRY

It's now the Fall of 2000, and there is another march on Washington, D.C. to protest the deterioration of our families and to unite ourselves over our common cause of family. I believe the march is being called with the purest of intentions, but marching on Washington is a tactic that has outgrown its usefulness. The nation's government can't stop the cause of our collective problem. Marching can't stop it. The problem I speak of is HATE. Not hate from the white people, but the hate among us, we African-Americans, and we African people worldwide.

We have had a renaissance of history in the last two decades. Amazing and startling truths about our collective past have been written and spoken about to all who care and dare to know the truth. Yet, all this history raises one of the most important of questions for us, "How did we get in this position, if we were the originators of all civilizations?"

My answer is HATE. Hate is the cause of all our problems. We have forgotten what we knew, and it is that one cause can have many different effects. This truth will forever elude those people who are content with observing, hypothesizing, theorizing, and fakin' it 'til you make it. Example: A rock is thrown in the middle of a lake; the rock goes in the water and vibrates 360 degrees. We've all seen this happen, and you can try this out in your kitchen sink. But, how many of us have connected this natural law to our condition?

This hate started millenniums ago. The Europeans are not the cause of our collective misery, we are. We've hated each other for sinturies. We taught the Europeans, and we taught them hate. We were envious of each other, and we turned to religions that justified jealousy and hate. If a person wasn't part of a particular religion, hating them was accepted and encouraged.

When we were whole, we knew that hate couldn't be tolerated in a society. This desire to enslave hate forever was the energy and cause of our civilizations. Not the accumulation of riches and fame, but the enslaving of hatred. Our monuments and ancient text shows and tells of our collective search for harmony and peace, and we knew that hate was the enemy of peace. But we became apathetic, and hatred grew in our hearts and eventually our actions started to reflect this hate. We fought wars with each other over the pettiest issues. We fought for land that from time immemorial we knew was all of ours. We started to sell ourselves for creature comforts, and eventually, entire tribes were sold into slavery by other Africans.

We no longer wanted to enslave Hate. We wanted to enslave our enemies, and our enemies were at one time our brothers and sisters. The women who have the babies became possessions to be bartered and sold. We became envious of each other. The hate grew to become a movement among us. We invented different languages to separate ourselves from each other. The thread that held us together was language, and we mutilated our sacred words and images, we started to have initiations to the truth - as if the truth needs an introduction.

When Europeans came off the shores of Europe, they were full of hate. The Moors taught them, and the Moors were Black Men and Women. We enslaved them because we could. We hated their pale skin, their odor, and their lack of civilization. We conquered them for over 7 sinturies. We were no longer the teachers of the world, but the tormentors of our brothers and sisters. We all come from Africa. Every human in this beautiful world comes from Africa. Black Men and Women are the fathers and mothers of all people, yet we became abusive parents because of our acceptance of hate.

To this very day of my writing these words, we continue to hate each other. We still haven't stamped out hate. Wars rage all over the world. There are people of all colors who profess that war is the final strategy. These people tell us that the goal of all the wars, i.e. military war, drug war, psychological war, chemical war, and war between the sexes, is peace. The only cause of peace is the enslavement of Hate. This Hate must be enslaved in our lifetime.

Plots of conspiracy and mayhem are rooted in hate. Hatred for others covered in laws. Can't we see that hatred leads nowhere, but to a more evil place? We Black people have suffered in the past 5 sinturies. Reparations are due for what was done to us, but before we get reparations from others, we must repair ourselves, This is Black business the healing of us. Tupac Shakur and Christopher "Biggie Smalls" Wallace, died because of hatred. Each spoke about hate - the hate they knew would kill them. Our generation is full of the hate we were taught while young. Stereotypical images, laws written to punish and destroy, and words of hate shouted over airwaves at each other. The old lies must die.

If we are not to pass this hatred onto the children, the education of them must reflect our new goal of the enslavement of hate. Deep inside we want peace, but hate must end.

We all inherited it, and we all must end it.

FREEDOM, MY WAY

I've had people ask me what is my religion, and I say, "Me." Religion is a word from the Latin language. It means to re-tie. This is why people go to church every week, to re-tie themselves back to God - back to the eternal. The word was meant to remind we humans that we are spirits in flesh who are traveling in space and time.

God is all of us, and inside of all of us. God is manifested in a billion different ways, but all is God. Like water in a stream, water in a faucet, and the water that nurtures the unborn child in the womb. All is water, but different at the same time.

This is the part of creation that eludes the slave master's medicine: we're all individuals, yet all the same. The universe will never be divided. We can play mind games, put God in the stars on high, and put ourselves on the ground separate from God, but the truth is eternal. God is alive in us. The healing begins when we start to believe this.

The only reality is that the impossible is always possible. There are those who want the world to stay the same, or they want to control the change that is inevitable. At one time, I wanted to change the world. I believed that white people were the cause of all the trouble. They may be the cause of the last 500 years of trouble, but the cause of the world's troubles is all of our faults. All people of all colors and of all nations on earth have contributed to this modern trouble. Therefore, we all share in its triumphs and failures.

As I stated, I wanted to change the world, but I learned that changing me is changing the world. Change comes one person at a time. Television creates social movements, but only conscious humans can sustain the movement. God is flowing in our veins. The more one believes this, the greater our world becomes.

The human spirit can never be enslaved or incarcerated. Slave masters come and go. History proves this. Only the truth remains. Many people in this "modern world" have attempted to hide and distort the truth, yet the truth is eternal. A truth 4,000 years ago is a truth today. Water was wet when the pyramids were built, and it's wet today. The truth is eternal.

I believed in the truth, and my body healed. By believing in God, the goodness and holiness of God, my soul healed. The body followed. Remember this brothers and sisters, heal the soul first and the body will follow. No matter what condition the body is in, or how painful the body aches. The soul is in worse shape. If the body is sick, the soul is sicker. Heal the soul first. A soul healed will automatically heal the body.

Don't give up on the world. I did this, and my soul gave up on this body it's in. This happens countless times with we humans. We give up on the world, and we leave the world kicking and screaming. Sometimes with our bodies filled with dis-ease.

Believe in the beauty - the simple beauty. When I was a child, my mother's voice made me smile. Waking up in the morning and seeing the Sun shine made me happy. I've lost more money and the things money buys than I can count. Still, I'm wealthy. Holy thoughts in my mind and heart insure that my wealth is infinite. I got enough to give the world. The more I give, the more I receive.

There is an Islamic saying, *"Take one step towards Allah, and Allah will take two steps toward you."* To me, this says that the universe (God, Allah) will always give you back more than you give. God is infinitely rich and giving.

If you give good, you will receive more good. Do bad, and you will receive more bad. We reap what we sow. Plant a small watermelon seed, and a few weeks later you will be given back a whole watermelon that will contain 100 more seeds.

Give Freedom, my way, a try.

Being Married

What I am dealing with right now in my life is raising a family. Raising a family has always been a challenge at anytime, and in any country. But being that I am an African-American man in 2001, it's even harder.

You see, my family and I have inherited the problems of our ancestors. My great-great grandparents were enslaved, and their parents before them were enslaved, and so on. The physical enslavement ended legally in 1863 with the signing of the Emancipation Proclamation, but like most laws, the crime didn't cease. We were never given land. We were never even given a dime of the wealth that we created. The ending of slavery didn't end the oppression it just caused the oppression to change in form, but stay true to its essence.

It's the Spring of 2001 here in Harlem. I look around, and I see the same shit going on. So, I've decided to start making changes.

All of my ancestors in this country have helped build, and sometimes died for America, which I'm sad to say is a euphemism for "a white man's world." We have worked long and hard, and still we don't have anything. We have some jobs, degrees, and a few material things, but of the real things, we don't have any. Real things like, physical freedom. We, I, still can't fully protect our family from the brutality of a human gone mad – a human who happens to be in a blue uniform.

Even though history shows that justice isn't blind, we are still subject to white and Black men from white suburbs coming into Harlem and arresting our Black children. Once a child is grabbed, we must go through their courts to seek their freedom. We are in a predicament, you see? One Black person's problem is all we Black folks' problem.

I'm married now with one son, by marriage, and another child in the womb waiting to be born. My wife believes, but when the bills start to come, her faith becomes weak. We argue. We scream at each other. She tells me to do something. I tell her, I am. She tells me it's not enough. The bills keep coming. I tell her that the only way we can free ourselves from being economic slaves of other people is that we must create our way.

I've been in many tight situations, and the only way I know to get some space is to open up my mind and heart, and let the God in me takeover. My wife sees the paper bills coming. I see nothing but the same old lies. I keep telling her that our problems are all in our minds, and the solution is also in our minds. And, that we choose which one we believe in. I will eternally choose the positive, but my wife gets worried. We argue constantly about this. I tell her to believe and trust in the goodness of creation, and the goodness that rests in our hearts. Success is like a seed. In order for it to grow, it must be nurtured. It must be believed in. Projecting failure, and letting others' threats overtake us is a sure death of our souls.

They do the same thing to us today that was done to our ancestors during our enslavement. They tell us we can't survive without them. Without them we are nothing. We will have no house, no water, no food, and no clothes. If we choose to believe in us, we will fail. This is what we Black people have been told since we set foot on this stolen land. Yet, we keep creating. We keep giving our souls to someone else's ever-greater glory. If we really gave our life to our Lord, we would be giving our life to ourselves. We would essentially be free, but we give our Sundays to the Lord, and all other days to the white world. Then we lament on Sunday about how things seem to be getting worse for us.

I tell my wife this, and she knows I speak the truth, but the bills drive her crazy with worry. Creating our own way is like creating a child. The first three months are rough. The woman is sick sometimes. Her body is going through changes, and she sometimes becomes irritable and down right angry with others. Still, Creation is on the move.

The world we live in is telling us that unless we have plenty of green pieces of paper with dead white men on it (money), the babies should be aborted. The media we watch is full of mayhem, crime, and injustices perpetuated by people of all colors. Someone, some group, something wants us all to be afraid. I say, the Sun rises and sets freely. The rain comes down for all. Food is given to whoever will plant and nurture the seed. But, what do I tell my wife when electricity, which is a product of nature, is a commodity? The rain is water, and water is freely given from the heavens, but we've been told we must pay. There is plenty of land in America, but we must pay for the land. This is the American way. Even if some of us get lucky in this economic lottery and purchase land, we must always pay taxes on the land. Therefore, we are all renters for life.

My wife sees all this, and she worries. It's hard for her to see the light sometimes because light costs, we're told. Still, I believe. And, I consciously choose what I believe in. I am a divine soul as you, the reader, are, and I choose to put my faith in me, in God.

I love my family dearly, and I will be of service to my race and all of humanity. Therefore, I have got to stay strong. You, the reader, have got to stay strong. I know there are millions upon millions of human souls of all colors who know we need a better way, but the better way will not come if we don't believe it will.

I tell my wife this, and we agree that the way is in our hearts, then another bill comes and the arguments start again. I visualize a better way. I dream of a Divine way. I consciously choose a better way. I've heard of faith breaking down walls and parting seas. I healed my body because of faith. In my lifetime, I've seen Apartheid end because of faith, so I gotta keep the faith, in faith. I wish I could take the pain out of our family growth, but the pain is a part of it.

I met my wife, Meru Nombeko Aisha Kheop, in the Fall of 1999 here in Harlem, New York at the Dr. John Henrik Clarke House on Convent Avenue. When I first saw her, she was strikingly beautiful to me, but most of all I felt a strength in her that I had never felt. It wasn't the strength of my mother or grandma. It was the strength of my wife.

We talked as we were given a brief tour by Dr. Leonard Jeffries. When the tour was over, we said good-bye to Dr. Jeffries, left together, and started walking on this unusually warm fall night. We walked from 138th and Convent Avenue to 116th Street and Malcolm X Boulevard. We went to Amy Ruth's on 116th Street for tea. The brother who owns the restaurant was there. He must have liked us because he was so welcoming and gave us a basket of delicious hot cornbread. The cornbread was almost better than my mama's cornbread!

We spoke for a good while in Amy Ruth's, then I walked her home and we spoke some more. When she walked into the building, I was left standing there hoping she would come back out and give a brother some more conversation. I called her when I got back to my studio, and we talked until 8 am.

In the weeks that followed, we talked more. She told me about her life, and I told her about my life and my troubled times. She had been married before, had a son named Cassius, and was living her life as best she could. She was the creator, producer and host of an educational program on cable for children ages 5 through 12, and had recently worked with the Black Panther Collective in Harlem where she helped them begin a clothing drive on 125th Street. She cared and was involved with Black people in the village of her birth, Harlem. Her daddy's mother and father raised all fourteen of their children right on 127th Street between Malcolm X Boulevard (Lenox Avenue) and Adam Clayton Powell Boulevard (7th Avenue). She went to elementary school on 127th Street and grew up in St. Nicholas projects. At sixteen she left New York to attend college in Northern California. Her journey led her to me.

I immediately trusted Meru. I told her the complete truth. Even the parts of my life that aren't so squeaky clean. I told her I had gotten not just my hands dirty, but also my whole body. But, regardless, my heart was as clean as the day I was born. I told her I hadn't been long out of Fort Dix, and that I was released on April 1, 1999. I hadn't been out for a year. At the time, I was on supervised release (federal probation) here in New York, and once again, it was on with the probation officer.

She understood me completely, and accepted me wholly. I digged this. She was further proof to me that dreams come true, that thoughts have power if we believe in our thoughts. Meru had studied Islam, and like me, she respected and cherished Islam, but was still searching. I told her my religion was me, and that my actions daily re-tied me to God with every step I take.

I met Cassius at the Schomberg Center here in Harlem. It was the evening of Henry Louis Gates' PBS Premier of his Africa series, and Meru invited me to attend with her along with Cassius, her sisterfriend, Karima, Karima's son, David, and herself.

Cassius was 7 years old then. He had a notebook with Pokemon cards. I had never heard of Pokemon at the time, so he joyfully educated me about the powers of his various Pokemon.

He was somewhat distant when we talked about other things. He was checkin' me out. His mother didn't date and he was serious about who he let get with her. Like his mother, Cassius is very bright, and has a way with drawing. The child can draw in a way that is a blessing.

Soon after that day, I asked Meru to marry me. She accepted, and we were married on

December 22, 1999 the first full moon in 333 years during the winter solstice. It was a special, intimate ceremony.

I was overjoyed to be married. I could see the end of the long tunnel I had been in for some time. Still, the federal courts weren't done with me, therefore I wasn't done with them. I was still on supervised release, and the probation officer was not my friend. When I was released from Fort Dix, I worked at a bookstore for a while to appease the courts. The courts like to see ex-convicts get a job in their machine. It shows them we are now rehabilitated, and that we accept life the way they make it. I had gone this far, and the way of righteousness had been good to me.

The courts didn't give a damn about me. So, I chose to embrace the holy way. I stopped working and got into politics. I decided to run for the office of Congressman of Harlem, New York in September of 1999. I could run for Congress because the office is a federal one,

and the Constitution of America regulates who can run. The age requirement is 25 years, and you must be a U.S. citizen. My having a criminal record couldn't stop this.

My opponent was Charles Rangel. He has been congressman for thirty years. He won the seat from Harlem legend, Adam Clayton Powell, Jr. I didn't think him a bad man, I just knew his time had come and gone. In Harlem, and throughout America, we young Black people have been under attack for years. The war on drugs is really a war on us. The only way for us to end this, and begin something new is to organize ourselves politically. We young Black people have tremendous power in America and the world. Our ghetto culture has become fabulous because we say so. Hip Hop is our news source, and far better and more timely than CNN.

I knew then, as I do now, that our politics must equal our cultural power. Campaigning is very hard, and even more difficult when you're trying to unseat a thirty-year veteran of politics. Still, he could be beat. We young people, and some older people, know that a great change is needed. The old tactics of protest aren't working. The prisons keep being built, and the police keep locking down more and more young Black and Brown men and women.

The laws of America are made by men and women, like myself. Government is just a word, and we humans define the word. There have been times when the word meant the power of the people collectively organized for the good of all the people. In America, the word government means protection of the rights and wealth of a few people. The rest of us must either get along, or be gone.

Millions upon millions of America's citizens are incarcerated. Many more millions are trapped in the corporate matrix. Still, the government "officials" tell us everything is going to be alright. Racism and the violence that comes from it aren't even discussed. Laws are made and passed that punish a person "after" they have violated another person's human rights. When the perpetrator is a corporation, the only punishment is a small payment of money.

Government must reflect the will of the people. Making certain plants and herbs illegal won't stop people from using it. Locking up millions of citizens hasn't stopped it. So, why keep incarcerating citizens? The same people who have outlawed these coca and marijuana plants are the same people who profit from the illegalization. Nothing is better for the increasing of demand and price of a commodity than the outlawing of a commodity.

Our nation has already tried a prohibition of liquor, and it was a great mistake. Now in 2001, certain drugs are illegal and millions of citizens are locked down. Still, people tell us that the next prison built will stop the drug dealing. Mayors tell the people we need a few more police officers and bigger guns, and the drug problem will stop. Congress and the Senate pass laws that encroach further and further on our human rights. For all purposes, the Bill of Rights is no more.

Government officials debate budgets while American children are killing each other in school cafeterias. Every social problem becomes a legal problem. The government said that drugs are being transported in cars, and the next step was the government passing a law giving police the right to stop citizens if the police officer thinks the car has drugs in it. And, of course the police are raised in America, and every American is touched by racism. So, it's only natural that police stop Black people most often. The media has told them that we Blacks are the cause of the nations decline. The schools present the world through the eyes of the European, who is the world's true minority because most of the earth's people are of color.

Mis-education and racism are as American as Jazz music, yet more laws are passed that will never solve the problems of today, therefore, the future is bleak. Still, the officials wonder why the children act so crazy.

I decided to run for Congress. I believed that I could not be ignored as Congressman, and therefore, we young Black and Brown people could not be ignored. I am a product of 20th century America, and like the millions who are young and Black, we are a power in this country. Our voice needs to be heard because I believe the solution is in the ghettos of America, not the suburbs. At one time it was the rural areas of America that had the answers. Then it was the cities of America. Now, it's the ghettos of America, which are filled with country people who came to the cities and now their children have the answers.

I was running for Congress while still on supervised release. Life was looking better. I was now the father of our Kheop House, and all that I had been through didn't seem to be in vain. My family believed that I was on a good course, and my mother was happy that campaigning didn't involve guns and violence, so she helped the campaign. My father and grandma were proud. My wife is a Sister born and raised in Harlem. Her father was born and raised in Harlem. Her mother's family is from North Carolina, but they moved here during the great migration north from the south.

The entire family, on both sides, was with me, but the Feds weren't feeling my campaign at all. I was suppose to be working for the system, not challenging it. And, if I was challenging it, I was supposed to be in the streets shooting at the police. I chose a different way, and they were pissed.

The probation officer started probation violation proceedings because I refused to stop campaigning and get a job. She, the probation officer, had determined with her supervisors that I couldn't possibly win, and that my campaign was a fraud. The Feds were trying to tell me which one of my ambitions was acceptable. I attempted to compromise for once with the Feds, but in the end, I had to go back to court in Washington, D.C.

Once again, I was back in front of Judge Lamberth. He told me I was wrong for not doing what the probation officer said do. He violated my probation, sentenced me to six months in a federal prison, but revoked my supervised release. This meant I would be through with them after serving the six months instead of continuing with the three years of supervised release. So, I won and loss.

I could not run for Congress at that time because six months out of action was too long, but upon release, I wouldn't be on supervised released anymore.

I went to jail on January 12, 2000, two weeks after Meru and I exchanged our vows. I was released on July 11, 2000. Election day was November 7, 2000. My ambition for an upset of Rangel and a new beginning for we young Black people was put on hold.

I was sent to Lewisburg Prison Camp in Lewisburg, Pennsylvania. I'm always amazed at how the small towns claim the prisons the way New Yorkers claim the Knicks. The camp was outside the wall of the Lewisburg Penitentiary. My wife visited regularly and gave me updates on the family. I read books and practiced patience. I was mad at being in prison again, but filled with God and all the future holds. On my day of release, my wife picked me up and I was back in Harlem by 1pm. It was a Sunny day. A blessing, I thought. All the other times I had been released, it was raining. So, life continues at the speed of life.

ZIMBABWE

The issue today throughout the Black world is one of Power. Economic power, political power, and social power, i.e. control of our culture and lives. But, there is one place in the world where the issue of power has been resolved with the solution of physical and spiritual action, that place is Zimbabwe.

As the world watches, the citizens of Zimbabwe are instituting their own form of reparations, a sort of grassroots reparations. The citizens of Zimbabwe for the past three weeks have forcibly been removing European farm owners from the land they have unjustly occupied for over a "sintury."

What does this mean to we African-Americans? It means the start of the final conflict. The conflict started when European and Arab invaders decided that African hospitality wasn't deserving of reciprocity. It started the day one of "them" took one of "ours" land by force and deceit. Since that day, it's been "on" between those of "us" who know and feel "our" land is "our" land! Not their land.

The action of the people in Zimbabwe is about the resolution of the land issue, i.e. the power issue. There can be no real freedom if a historical aggressor and a present day oppressor of the children control the land. When you have land, you can feed yourself and your loved ones. When you don't have land, you ask for food from those who have the land. If those who have control of the land hearts are set in profit, the product of the land – food - will become a commodity.

In other words, more hungry children means the higher the prices for what is needed - food. Therefore, greater profit for the landowners for what they desire - things. While the rest of us struggle to eat.

Removing Europeans from the land in Zimbabwe has sent shock waves throughout the European world. The reason for the shock waves is the righteous actions of the people of Zimbabwe.

Throughout the world, Europeans have stolen land from the original people of that land. Outside of europe proper, there is no place they occupy that is rightfully theirs, and even their occupation of europe could be contested through the use of historical data.

Through mis-education, deceit, and the setting up of unjust laws and courts to administer their hypocrisy of words, they have manipulated the Black world for over five sinturies.

But all things change, and the universe is a just place. No empire can survive when its life comes at the expense of so many other people's death.

The mentality of aggression whether colonialism, imperialism, or neo-colonialism is coming to an end. It has served its purpose for the world. The mentality of aggression has shown the world that aggression and deceitfulness leave the victim of the aggression, and the aggressor, without a heart. The victims and the aggressor's heart have been lost in the justifying of the original crime of taking what wasn't theirs.

So, we Americans-Americans, young and old, must choose now! The world is in the middle of change; we are at the crossroads of change. Will we side with those who seek to maintain the status quo (European supremacy)? Or, will we side with our brothers and sisters in Zimbabwe who are acting in the most divine way?

The European propaganda press will start to report the divine actions of the people of Zimbabwe in their press (newspapers, magazines and television). They will try and convince us that there is a better way to solve the issues of land ownership, i.e., power. Without a doubt, the "right way, better way" will be through lawsuits and non-violent protest. They will present so-called reasons why the seizing the land of Europeans, who stole the land, is wrong. They will attempt to prove to us that they, Europeans, are not bad people. It's the "impatient people of Zimbabwe" who are bad. They will talk of human rights violations and the break down of the rule of law in Zimbabwe. They will say President Robert Mugabe is a bad leader for not protecting the Europeans from the rightful owners of the land that they, the Europeans, stole. They will attack Zimbabwe in the economic arena. They may try and starve the people through an economic embargo, but ALL THIS WILL FAIL!

Europeans are one tenth of the world's population, and can no longer rule the world. The economic and political rule of Europeans is based on deceit and lies, and no lie can live forever. They, the Europeans, will attempt to fight, but they will lose. I see the future; I see the demise of an unjust, cruel, and ungodly idea. I see the end of European supremacy.

MISREPRESENTED DESTINY

I just saw Spike Lee's masterpiece "Bamboozled". The movie is off the chain!

My wife and I liked the film so much we went and bought the soundtrack today.

The soundtrack is brilliant, but one song stands out to me, and that's Stevie Wonder's "Misrepresented People". The song speaks on how this European world has misrepresented we African-Americans, and African people world wide. They misrepresented our history and thought they could misrepresent our destiny.

By our destiny I mean, our destiny as a completely free people. Freedom to me means being free of the chains of hate and racism. We all deserve a world free of this evil that is planted in our hearts and minds from birth.

I was born black in America 33 years ago. The seeds of hatred are planted early in our nation. Even though my parents didn't want these seeds to be planted in my young self, how could they avoid it when our country saw me, the young black citizen, as a future menace? One to be trained away from my destiny of freedom from evil that manifests in this world in more ways than my mind can dream of. Yo! I was born an outlaw.

So, here I sit in the 2nd millennium of we Africans lost in the space of European history. Misrepresented destiny never happened because we never forgot. We may have taken a few detours, but we never forgot our collective destiny, which is: the return to freedom. But, how can we have freedom with hatred thriving in the land of our birth?

It is the challenge of life to beat back hatred in the heart. It is forever trying to break in the heart. It will squeeze in the smallest of holes like a rat in the middle of winter. It wants in your house.

We challenge hatred when we accept responsibility for our personal actions, and we take actions in the present to correct the wrongs of the past. We Black people are owed reparations for sure. We have got to get that, Black people. The world can't be free of hatred until this world respects the past and settles the past problems. We have got to get radical now. We have got to embrace the real us - the part of us that gets pissed when we hear about another Black soul executed on some city street in the land of our birth.

We have got to fire ourselves up now. Not RIOT HOT, but build a new world on the ashes of the one hatred built HOT.

REPARATIONS

The premise that what happened in the distant "past" somehow does not effect the "present" is a faulty one. Time is not a quantity, but a quality. Time can be "good time" and time can be "bad time," but all time is connected whether good or bad.

Some critics say we African-Americans shouldn't raise the argument of reparations because the cause for the need of reparations - slavery - happened long ago and cannot possibly affect the present. We should move on and forget the past.

Using the premise that what happened in the distant past does not effect the present, we can assume that the Constitution of our country is irrelevant because it happened in the distant past, and no one alive participated in the writing of the Constitution. As a matter of fact, all medical research should be discarded because all medical research is based upon the success and failures of the past.

Our judicial system should be ignored because it is based on "case law" which says that legal cases of the "past" can be used to support legal cases of the "present." Also, all crimes can be forgotten if the perpetrator isn't caught the instant of the offense.

Let me use another example to make my point. A man and a woman have a house. The house contains the accumulated possessions of countless generations. This also includes the accumulated wealth of the family. By wealth I don't just mean material, but spiritual wealth. You see, the house is their HOME. Now, some bandits come and rob the house. Not only do the bandits steal the material wealth, they steal the spiritual wealth. The bandits stole the Children of the house. Now these bandits prosper from the crime. They not only prosper materially, but spiritually.

By spiritually, I mean this: when we were brought here to America, we brought the greatness of Africa with us. We came as slaves, but we built a nation like Africans. Our ideas and genius for civilization were used, but all that our souls produced was stolen for over four sinturies.

This ill-gotten prosperity is passed on from generation to generation. Not once has the rightful owner of the original stolen wealth been compensated for the crime. The victim has never been made whole. The Europeans attempted to mis-educate us away from our destiny, and attempted to manifest our destiny for themselves. Feel me, young Black people? You cannot manifest your destiny if you don't know who you are. You are not the descendants of slaves. You are descendants of African Men and Women who fought slavery every inch of the way to our freedom. And, your freedom cannot begin until you know who you are - a divine descendant of greatness and truth.

The foundation of American Law is restitution. When someone steals something, the person must repay or return what was stolen or that person is sent to prison to repent for his or her crime. What happens if the original crime has never been prosecuted? Then the crime continues. The sins of the Fathers and Mothers are passed on if the original victim was never compensated.

So, here in the "present" we descendants of the original victims, and the descendants of the original criminals, are still dealing with the original crime. Reparations make the victims whole. What was stolen must be returned. Laws outlawing future crimes are just, but empty if reparations for the original crime have not been paid.

The debate that is raging here in the "present" concerning reparations shows how needed they are. There can be no peace in America until we African-Americans have been made whole. No social programs or income transfer programs will help. The "past" proves this.

Reparations are just in this case, and the acceptance of the crime can absolve the criminals and move our nation forward.

BELIEF IS THE KILLER

I write this to raise a valid question, is the AIDS virus causing death, or is it the propaganda of European science and followers of their medical science?

Europeans have dominated the medical field for over 5 sinturies. Their medicine is rooted firmly in their mentality, which is based on velocity and quantity. By velocity, I mean speed. They believe that anything that is made to go faster is a technological breakthrough. They also believe that size and quantity somehow equates with success. The bigger and faster something is, the better it is.

This mentality is the essence of their medicine, yet it's wrong because it's cerebral. They are too much in their heads, and too far from their hearts. A human body is more than just a body. It is a spirit encased in a body. To start from the premise that the body can be healed by ignoring the spirit is backwards and barbaric. In such an environment, surgeons and pharmaceutical pills become the healers.

Whenever any pharmaceutical company researches a new medicine, they have clinical trials. In these trials they give the pill or capsule of medicine that they invented to one group of people. Then they give another group of people a "placebo" which is a flour pill. The same flour that your mother uses to cook is compressed into a pill or capsule. No one person knows which pill they have. All assume they have the pharmaceutical pill or capsule. Now, you may ask why introduce a "placebo" into medical research? Because their scientists know that the human spirit has a capacity to heal itself and the body it is inside of. It's a huge con game, a scam that has survived far too long.

The "placebo" always gets equal or better results than the medicine. They'll always try and lie that their pill is effective, but they know that it's all belief. If a person believes in the doctor and her or his ability to heal them, they will be healed.

AIDS is a massive form of propaganda. Propaganda in that, the AIDS virus is said to be the cause of death for millions of humans, in general, and Africans in particular. Their medicine is the real voodoo. It's all smoke and mirrors. They use speed and quantity to fool a person and sometimes a nation. The game they run is this: The so-called pill they give a person is suppose to stop the pain quickly, which feeds into the need for relief from pain, but it's not the pill that heals, it's the belief in the person prescribing the pill. Then, if a person has doubts, they roll out the large quantity of "scientific research" to get the desired effect, which is belief in them, the European.

This is the same con game they've been running for "sinturies." The word disease broken down to its essence reveals the true meaning of the illness. Dis-Ease. "Dis" means not well, disturbed. "Ease" means comfort, at peace. The word disease is in reference to the spirit, not the body. This is the part of African medicine that couldn't be grasped by the Greeks. It is based on the spirit, not the body. The spirit must be put at ease - not the body.

Following a lost soul will yield only negative and heartless results. Haven't we people of color learned from our recent history that the European is lost, and fakin' it until he/she hopefully makes it? The western media propagated for over a year that the world would end if their computers couldn't read 2000 from 1999. They actually had the world in a panic. People believed that the sun wouldn't rise and the universe would implode because a computer malfunctioned. Fortunately, the heavens laugh at such foolish intellectual adventures.

The cure for AIDS lies behind our morbid belief in Europeans. The cure for AIDS is the cure for the nation, for the world. A conscious mind alone cannot uncover the truth. Only a conscious heart can reveal that which truly heals, that which lives eternally. That "it" inside of us that has delivered us to this present day in hope that we'll make tomorrow better.

Although we now communicate over a device that was invented out of the western mentality - the internet - remember that technology cannot heal. Technology can only amplify the thoughts of the user. Let us start to amplify the thoughts of our hearts and leave this downward spiral of belief in magicians with degrees. AIDS isn't the killer, belief is.

BLACK AND WHITE

Many are saying the historical events taking place in Zimbabwe are about black and white. They see Africans forcibly removing Europeans from the stolen land they have occupied for over a sintury, and assume it's about hating white humans.

The issue is about justice. It's about action with substance - words of freedom backed by hearts in action.

The tactics of protest and the appealing to the humanity of the Europeans is ended. They do not hear us. They interpret protest, lawsuits, and speeches as weakness. They feel triumphant right now. As police brutalize we African-Americans daily, they laugh at us. A covert war on drugs has become an overt war on young Black men and women. They use their laws to incarcerate us for years, and they justify the hypocrisy by hiding their true intentions of destruction in so-called community righteousness.

As we struggle, they thrive. As we die slowly, they grow stronger. But still, this isn't about a black and white thing. If we allow ourselves to fall into this faulty way of thinking, we will be trapped again in a web of deceit.

We cannot ignore the millions of Black people who will side with the European when the issue of maintaining European supremacy is challenged. Their lives are tied to the master/employer. These lost African souls see no world beyond Europeans. They feel no pain other than the pain of their European masters/employers. In their minds, they lie to themselves. With their mouths, they cause dissension among us.

We must have a unified idea. The idea should be complete control of "our" lives. To achieve this, we must have unity. Now, the Black servants of European power will start to do their thing, do what they are paid the big bucks to do! Divide us. To divide means to reduce the whole through division. Divide 4 by 2, you get the lower number of 2. Keep dividing and eventually you move into the world of negative numbers. The united whole is no more.

We now have a unified idea, complete control of "our" lives. No more lies, prisons, brutality, mis-education, false gods, no more shit. Now, to stop us and to continue the assault of our babies, we must be divided. How they will attempt to divide us is by presenting alternative ideas through the mouths of their Black servants/employees. The puppets will present more ideas that we should consider, more ways of action. They will tell us that they are adding to our unified idea, thereby creating a greater idea. But this is deceit.

They will attempt to divide the unified idea. In Zimbabwe, the people are acting in a unified way. The entire world is watching. All of

Black Africa, Asia, Australia, South America, Latin America, all are watching. The Black mouthpieces will say the goal is correct, but the method is incorrect. They will present ideas that will stall the rise of righteousness. They will attempt to do this until the original idea of "complete control of our lives" has been reduced to, "Can we all just get along?"

Divide and conquer, once conquered, continue to divide the conquered. This is such a hateful philosophy. Our neighborhoods, our states, our nation, our motherland, our world has been divided long enough. We must keep our eyes on the prize. Each and every African-American who feels for their children must stay focused. We multiply and increase the power of the idea with our belief in the idea of complete control of our lives. We divide and reduce the idea when we allow doubt and fear to set in. We must be brave. The world has not always been like this, no matter what their holy books say. We were before their books, and we'll live beyond their books.

The truth is inside our hearts. The way will be opened with our hands and feet acting in harmony with the universe. They will try and scare us. Tell us how strong and organized they are. Their Black mouthpieces will reinforce the ideas of their greatness.

Belief in us is all we need. A new world can be created in the blink of an eye.

LET THE TEACHERS TEACH

It's being said that the children in Harlem, New York City's School District #5, and Black neighborhoods worldwide, cannot learn at the pace of the rest of the world. In the newspapers they tell tales of horror about our neighborhoods, but they don't live here.

Most of the young children on our block of 131st Street attend Community School 133, which is at the corner of 5th Avenue in New York City. This school is staffed by mostly Black Women and Men, and against all odds the teachers and administrators prepare our children for the forces of this world that hope they become another negative statistic.

The school board has come up with a plan they say will cure the ills of children not passing on to the next grade. That plan is called New Standards. The standards are minimum requirements that each child must possess to pass on to the next grade. The way they seek to discover if "our" children meet their standards is by giving the children a series of tests throughout the school year.

But, the tests are written as if the world we live in is fair and just. New York City is full of racism and hatred. It's not nice to say, I know, but it's real brothers and sisters. Hatred is not enslaved in New York City, and we Black people are the first victims of hatred in New York City.

Our children are the youngest of all victims. Our history is misrepresented in the history books the children are taught from. We as a people are misrepresented throughout the educational system of New York City.

The teachers are forced to teach a curriculum that will not prepare our children to be a real person. A person knowledgeable of their true history, and therefore, knowing their true destiny. No, our children are lied to then tested to see how many of the lies they can remember.

They represent our children as slow learners in the popular daily newspapers of New York City, and the world. Children will learn if what they are learning has a purpose beyond getting a job in a world full of hatred.

The goal of our children's learning must be to end this hatred and evil in the world they were given. Only the truth can free their hearts to create new ways of living and loving. These standard tests are cold and heartless, and prove nothing but the stupidity of hate. Teach the children of Harlem, and the world, the truth about the history of the world, then we will see the change in our neighborhoods that we have been praying and wishing for. Teach the children that it was Black people who taught Europe the ways of civilization. It was Black men and women who taught the world to sail the world. Teach them that all mathematics comes from their ancestors. Teach them that all religions come from their homeland of Africa.

Our vision for our children must grow now, if we are to grow. Allowing other people to continue to lie to us, and our children, will give us the results lies are meant to achieve. That result is we lose our way by following the lie.

The Awakening

Slowly and methodically did my mind climb
out of the depths of ignorance.
So many battles fought with doubt and
hesitation.
My soul has left countless carcasses of fantasies
and lies on battlefields that stretch across the
eternity of creation.
Steady climbin' and fightin'.
Searching in the wilderness of creation -
moving and living the lies until the truth is
revealed.
Behind the many masks has my soul hid behind,
afraid to embrace the truth of its destiny.
Running throughout the sinturies from one
dream to the next.
Fulfilling prophecy of countless generations of
wandering souls trying to find their way home.
I hear stories of the past and see monuments
built by those no longer breathing.
Yet, the stories I know and feel here, in the
present.
The monuments bring back to life those who've
gone on.
Some I remember, most I can't recall.
How accessible is reality to those who dream in
reality?
How can a soul see when the eyes only have
sight for the fantasy?

What happens when too many dream, even
when awake?
"Liberation for all souls!" I shout.
But the dreamers mistake my war cry for a
death call.
The Lord looked out unto eternity and saw
itself, felt itself, and from itself came myself.
Never separated am I from that which created
me - the wonderful Creator who gave me the
power to create so that it could live through my
creation.
The more complicated the sound,
the more simplistic and primal the feeling.
How long have I wanted to go home, but
momma told me home was where the heart is,
and the heart is always in the living moment.
So, I'm always home.
As a matter of fact, I never left.
I've just been discovering the boundaries of
eternity.
I met her, my wife, in a nice place.
I heard her voice before I saw her face.
I only came because I was called, but stayed
because of her.
What is power but the ambition of the
powerless?
If one tries to catch it, it gets caught.
But once caught, it burns.
Yet, the burn can consume or bring new life.
Who decides who gets consumed, and who gets
reborn?
I say only the one who becomes the Power.

How Do We Start to Live?

The most difficult drama that a human will bear witness to, is the drama of life. How does a person remember he or she is ONE? That God lives inside the temple that invites GOD? There is GOD in the sky. There is GOD on Earth. There is GOD in YOU. There is GOD in all.

If you believe my words, and embrace the truth of your existence, then you will have evolved. I say, “my words,” because I have not a doubt or a reason for my existence. I simply live, and have not a doubt I am eternal. I search for no reason to my existence. I exist and don't hesitate to advance on the truth. Illusions carved in words mean nothing to me. I use my senses the way a president or king uses his army. I let my body flow.

My thoughts are minimal because my thoughts are at my service. All my mind can do is make decisions based on the senses - touch, sight, taste, sound, and smell. Allowing my mind, which believes in the senses, to guide me through eternity would be the equivalent of a king or president allowing the spies, the intelligence, to make decisions on the information that they, the spies (the mind) have gathered.

To be conscious of existence is what is attainable for all lost souls, yet so many believe it is good to make a home in hell. By hell, I mean that vibe, that energy, which is created when a part of creation believes itself to be separate from all creation - separate from the Creator.

This is the hell that so called dis-eases of the spirit (soul) are misdiagnosed as a virus in the body. Nothing outside the body can influence the internal harmony of the human who is aware that he or she is a perfect model of heaven. What makes the heart beat? Is it batteries? Electricity? Gas? Can a person's soul be burned, drowned, shot, or stabbed? I say, "No." Yet, we live because of this eternal energy inside of all of us. We are built by God, and powered by God. WE live eternally when we acknowledge we are all connected to God in the most intimate of ways. We are the Temple.

This energy source is unquantifiable and unidentifiable. It doesn't leave footsteps. Not even in its chemical analysis does it reveal itself. DNA mapping is more European intellectual adventures.

The spirit can be analyzed by any human that chooses to look in the mirror. What you see is what spirit built. Not German built, not Japanese built, not made in the USA, but made in the mind of the spirit that is being reflected in the mirror.

They say that AIDS is a virus that attacks the body's immune system. Over time this virus is suppose to be so effective in waging a chemical war on the body that the body will collapse in fatigue and will fall victim to exhaustion. Then the body meets its demise.

How can the energy, the 'it' that makes the human heart pump and be attacked by a chemical from earth when no chemical can attack the spirit? But it can cause doubt in the mind, and then begins the war for the body. A person's soul isn't of this world. It simply engages all that the senses put before it, and lets all forms of spirit exist, and all spirit is inside of all forms.

All who follow the lost human souls that blindly follow "sinturies" of GODless existence will die in the paleness of ignorance and fear. These lost souls have believed in their illusions. Now, the world of our common existence has been lost too, yet the heaven that has been written so elaborately about in so-called ancient times, is ever coming and going. The spirit flows through all time and all material. Heaven is here for those who acknowledge their own divinity.

The doubters, intellectuals, law enforcers, and law supporters, will definitely suffer in this life, and others, for what will seem like an eternity until an evolution of consciousness comes. And, only the mind and spirit existing in peace and harmony will cause an evolution of consciousness.

Brothers and Sisters, the world can be recreated. The way nature will destroy the Spring of 2001, it will recreate another in 2002.

Nothing in the universe is unchanging, except the spirit that exists eternally, the spirit that moves the heavens, changes the seasons, makes the sun rise and set, that makes our hearts pump, the spirit that brought Africans through the dying season (slavery, colonialism, and neo-colonialism). The only sacrifice that is acceptable to this spirit, this eternal soul I represent in the flesh, is the sacrifice of our illusions. The world can be renewed because of the will of the spirit that is inside all of us. Don't try and name it, just feel it. One person at a time does heaven start to invade the thoughts of humans.

It is all in our minds, this eternal suffering that has so many trying to kiss ass to get to heaven. There is no ass to kiss in reality. No super authority figure, no laws, just existence.

So let us rally for a new world - a just and righteous world. Not a rally to protest the old world that hate built. Let us be brave and courageous. Let us flow like the water. Let us fight like fire in a dry forest. Let us dream like the wind that is free to move on all levels. I wish the peace of eternity for all of you who are a part of me, and I a part of you.

Live Free. Die Free.

Do it all over again in Peace.

"Although they knew God, they did not glorify him as God or give thanks, but became vain in their reasoning, and their senseless minds have been veiled. For while professing to be wise, they became fools, and they change the glory of the incorruptible God for an image made like the corruptible man."

-Tehuti, on the decline of Egypt 330 B.C.

ACKNOWLEDGEMENTS

I give thanks to the eternal and ever living God that lives inside of me, and everything and everyone else. Thank you to my mama, June Elaine Johnson, my father, Ronald Edward Johnson, and my grandma, Dorothy Ruth Smith. Thank you my wonderful wife, Meru Nombeko Aisha Kheop, and to Cassius Stephen Naylor, my stepson, for reminding me that I was a little boy once. Thank you to my younger brothers Maurice Johnson and Ronald Johnson Jr. Thank you to all my aunts, uncles and cousins. Thank you to my in-laws, the Gaddie and Dixon families.

Thank you to the Cahills and Browns. Thank you for the knowledge of self Dr. Yosef Ben-Jochannan, Dr. John Henrik Clarke, Reverend Charles Kenyatta, Dr. Donn Davis, Dr. Alvin Thornton, Dr. James Milton, Sister Carol, Ms. O'Donald, and Dr. Chiek Anta Diop. Thank you to Kevin Cahill, Dale Brown, Rodney Palmer, Jeff Parks, Kevin Bivens, Jill Lewis, Franchelle Colbert, Charyl Pitts and the Pitts family, Arnold Griffith, Carlos Cee Rodriguez, Elohiem, Pete Henry, Universal, Divine, Naim, I.B. Imperial, Suge, Corey, all my young guns and souljahs of all colors and races.

Thank you to all my ancestors. Because of you, there is a Me – a We. Rest in eternal peace, and please accept this book as an eternal offering to all of you. I would also like to say thank you to all the cities and countries I've visited in my life so far. I've been to almost every state in America. I've been to a couple of Caribbean nations, and I've travelled to the motherland, Africa.

I wish all the people that I've met from around the nation and the world, Peace, Life, Health, Wealth, and Strength.

Sincerely,
Michael Abdullah Kheop

www.ingramcontent.com/pod-product-compliance
Lightning Source LLC
LaVergne TN
LVHW050641100826
845148LV00011B/1936

* 9 7 8 0 6 1 5 3 8 0 9 9 5 *